50 WAYS COACHES CAN CHANGE THE WORLD

• •

C.J. HAYDEN

Wings for Business, LLC
San Francisco, CA

This book is designed to provide information in regard to the subject matter covered. It is sold with the understanding that the author and publisher are not engaged in rendering legal, accounting, or other professional service. If expert assistance is required, the services of a competent professional should be sought. The author and publisher shall have neither liability nor responsibility to any person or entity with respect to any loss or damage caused, or alleged to have been caused, directly or indirectly, by the information contained herein.

If you do not wish to be bound by the above, you may return this book to the publisher for a full refund.

Published by Wings for Business, LLC
P.O. Box 225008 • San Francisco, CA 94122
www.wingsforbusiness.com

ISBN-10: 0615623476
ISBN-13: 978-0615623474

$1 from each copy sold will be donated to the International Coach Federation Foundation, www.foundationoficf.org

Printing/manufacturing information for this book may be found on the last page.

Never doubt that a small group of thoughtful, committed citizens can change the world. Indeed, it is the only thing that ever has.
– Margaret Mead

CONTENTS

· ·

INTRODUCTION

● ●

Are you ready to change the world? If you're like most of the coaches I know, you think it needs some changing! As citizens, we have a vision of how things should be, for our government, economy, society, and the environment. As coaches, we hear from our clients and colleagues every day about change that desperately needs to occur. And as changemakers – because that's who coaches truly are – we want to make it all happen.

In this book, you'll get to know your tribe – coaches who not only believe the world needs to change, but are working to change it right this moment. You'll recognize ways of building a better world that you're already practicing, find new approaches you haven't yet tried, and learn about people, places, and tools to help you implement what you discover.

There are many ways you can make use of this book:

- Find inspiration for your world-changing desires
- Identify new resources to help implement your changemaking goals
- Validate that you're already on the right track
- Locate others who are on the same path
- Launch a new world-changing project of your own

In the back of the book, you'll find a "How to Get Started" chapter, which will help you determine which of the book's ideas you might like to act on, and how.

I hope that you will also consider one more possibility, which is to discuss the ideas in this book with other coaches. I've provided suggested discussion questions as an appendix, which can be used with a book study group or any coaching community. You can also post comments and queries on the book's companion website, and explore there what other readers have said.

One important note – this book contains many website addresses, which were valid at the time of publication. But URLs change quickly, and you may also find it easier to access them via active links than to type them into your browser. On the book's companion website, you can log in to the readers' area and find up-to-date, clickable URLs. If you find a URL in the book that no longer works, please check the site for an update.

I've tried to include a variety of perspectives in this book, and you'll see coaches quoted from around the world and from many different backgrounds, as well as resources from multiple countries. The majority of resources, however, are from the U.S., Canada, and the United Kingdom, which are the areas best known to me.

If you have additional resources you'd like to suggest, please visit the book's website and tell us about them. You're also invited to share your own story of changemaking there.

For each copy of this book sold, one dollar is donated to the International Coach Federation Foundation, making coaching and coach training available to those who can't afford it. That's one more way this book can help coaches promote change.

Thank you for supporting this project. I look forward to hearing more from you as we all change the world together.

C.J. Hayden, San Francisco, CA
www.coacheschangetheworld.com

PART I:
CHANGE THE WORLD
AS A CITIZEN,
EMPLOYEE, OR
BUSINESS OWNER

● ●

First and foremost, coaches are citizens of their communities, countries, and the planet we all share. The majority of us are independent business owners, while others work within organizations as employees.

Each of these roles gives us many opportunities to change the world. When we act to make a difference as a citizen, employee, or business owner, we are serving as role models to our clients and our communities. "Walking our talk" in this way allows us to be more effective coaches, leaders, and changemakers in any sphere we choose.

1. Offer a portion of your coaching services pro bono.

● ●

Give the gift of coaching to deserving people and organizations who can't afford to pay.

Not everyone who could benefit from coaching can afford it. People and organizations who are disadvantaged, at-risk, or doing good work in the world may need coaching the most, but be least able to pay for it. Your coaching can make a powerful contribution to the planet if you commit to giving some of it away.

As a whole, coaches probably give away more of their professional time than people in most other fields. But, they don't always have a clear design for this pro bono work. They may be coaching people for free who could actually afford to pay a fee. And, some self-employed coaches may be giving away too much coaching for the health of their own businesses.

Make a plan for your pro bono coaching.

1. Designate a percentage of your coaching time that you're willing to provide at no charge. This gives you both a goal to strive for and an upper limit to keep your altruistic tendencies under control.
2. Decide who you would most like to benefit from your pro bono work. Select a target market to serve, just as you would to pursue paying clients.
3. Reach out to people and organizations in the market you've chosen, offering coaching for free, with no strings attached. Be proactive rather than reactive to find the pro bono clients you most desire.

Look for opportunities to offer pro bono coaching through organizations like these:

The Coach Approach
www.coachapproachinc.org

The Coach Initiative
www.coachinitiative.org

International Coach Federation Foundation
www.foundationoficf.org

SupporTED
www.thehf.org/SupporTED.html

Women for Change Coaching Community
www.w4c3.org

"I'm a passionate evangelist of pro bono coaching because I dream of a worldwide 'coaching culture,' where most people have basic coaching skills, conversations are supportive and respectful, and having a coach is as common as having a dentist. I recommend offering the gift of coaching not only to those who cannot pay, but to executives and thought leaders. Once they experience coaching, they become coaching advocates for themselves, their organizations, their families, and society."

Ruth Ann Harnisch, president of the Harnisch Foundation in New York, NY, has directed millions in grants to coaching-related philanthropies.

2. Volunteer for causes you believe in.

● ●

Coaches are also citizens; offer any of your skills and talents to initiatives you care about.

Every social cause could use more help, and you have many useful abilities beyond your coaching skills. Your service could benefit organizations ranging from a local nonprofit or school to a national cause or global initiative. You can contribute your professional skills, personal talents, or just an extra pair of hands.

Volunteering doesn't benefit only those receiving your services; it also can have benefits for you:

- Make new contacts valuable for your business or career.
- Gain professional experience to add to your resume or portfolio.
- Improve your communication, interpersonal, and organization skills.
- Learn first-hand about the issues that concern you.
- Make new friends from diverse backgrounds who share your interests or values.
- Be part of your community, inspire others, and feel good about how you're spending your spare time.

Volunteer for a worthy cause doing work you enjoy.

1. Consider what skills or interests you might like to make use of or explore in your volunteer time.
2. Identify the type of cause or initiative that would most appeal to you.
3. Determine what you'd like to gain as a result of your volunteer experience.

4. Evaluate how much time you can contribute, on a one-time basis or as ongoing service.
5. Seek out opportunities that would offer an intersection of the four elements above.

These organizations help volunteers find opportunities:

All for Good
www.allforgood.org

HandsOn Network
www.handsonnetwork.org

Idealist
www.idealist.org

VolunteerMatch
www.volunteermatch.org

"Volunteering and coaching have a lot in common: both require us to engage in meaningful conversations, ask difficult questions, and act on inspiration. Believing that people are capable of transforming themselves and the world is the reason I do both. By volunteering, I've gained skills, confidence, friends, an expanded world view, and the certainty that individuals can and do make a difference. All around the world, volunteers strengthen and reinforce the best in people. So do coaches."

Martha Willson coaches professionals in career transition. She serves on the board of Volunteer Calgary in Alberta, Canada.

3. Donate a percentage of your coaching income to charity.

● ●

Whether it's your personal income or that of your business, set aside a percentage to donate each year.

Good causes need money to get their job done in the world. You don't have to give much to start making a difference. Designating a percentage of your coaching income for charitable donations allows you to give more as your income grows, while still contributing a minimum even when your earnings are low.

Making charitable donations can make a contribution to you, too:

- Make a fun project out of selecting your charities. You can also involve your kids, employees, or clients.
- Take an income tax deduction if you're eligible.
- When you give a substantial amount, you or your business may receive public recognition.
- Feel rewarded that your hard work is helping to make the world better, even when you're just doing your regular job.

Make a charitable giving plan for yourself or your business.

1. Choose a percentage to donate that works for you. Helpful guidelines: the average American donates 2% of their income each year, Canadians and British donate about 1%. The benchmark for socially responsible businesses to donate is often cited as 1% of gross income or 5% of net profits.

2. Identify charities that match your values and interests. You might select a new one each year, or a group of several you give to consistently. Or choose one local, one national, and one global cause.

If you're not sure where to give, here are some coaching-related charities to consider:

The Brande Foundation Coaching Project
www.thecoachingproject.org

Coaching the Global Village
www.coachingtheglobalvillage.org

Laura Whitworth Prison Project
www.prisonproject.org

Pro bono coaching organizations, page 3

"At my coaching firm, we delight in donating a significant portion of profit to charities we believe make a difference in the world. Each year we select two charities – last year we chose to send £24,000 to WYSE International and Kakunyu School in Uganda. We also commit a proportion of our time to pro bono work within charities whose projects we believe in, including offering coaching and time in support of our chosen charities."

Charles Brook, London, England, is founder and managing director of TPC (The Performance Coach). His international organization dedicates 10-15% of profits to charities each year.

4. Give back to the coaching community.
●●●●●●●●●●●●●●●●●●●●●●●●●●●●●

Contribute your time, money, or expertise to support the field of coaching as it supports you.

The coaching community provides you with business and career resources, education, camaraderie, and peer support. Consider giving back to your community in one of the following ways.

For coaching associations, chapters, or networking and special interest groups, serve on a board or committee, or give a talk or workshop. Organizations include:

Association for Coaching (U.K.)
www.associationforcoaching.com

Co-Active Network Niche Communities
www.coactivenetwork.com

Coach U Special Interest Groups
www.coachinc.com/CoachU/SIG/

International Association of Coaching
www.certifiedcoach.org

International Coach Federation
www.coachfederation.org

For coaching publications and social networks, write an article, column, or blog post. Publications include:

Choice: The Magazine of Professional Coaching
www.choice-online.com

Coaching: Journal of Theory, Research & Practice
www.tandf.co.uk/journals/rcoa

Coaching at Work
www.coaching-at-work.com

International Coach Federation Coaching World
www.icfcoachingworld.com

International Journal of Mentoring and Coaching
www.emccouncil.org.uk

For coaching charities, volunteer your time or make a donation. Charities include:

Pro bono coaching organizations, page 3

Coaching charities, page 7

"If you want to make a real difference in the world, look in your own backyard. Today's strong and vibrant coaching community rests squarely upon the shoulders of thousands of volunteer coaches who contribute their time and expertise to create, nurture and lead the diverse coaching community we call home. And here's the amazing thing. What begins as a small contribution in your own backyard can turn into a global gift."

Kay Cannon is an award-winning executive coach in Lexington, KY. She served as the 2007 president of the International Coach Federation.

5. Buy sustainable, fair trade, or used products, then donate them for re-use.

• •

Reduce your impact on the planet and its people by choosing what you buy and re-using what you can.

M odeling socially responsible behavior allows you to demonstrate your commitment to your clients, other coaches, and the communities to which you belong. Send a message of social responsibility by buying sustainable, fairly produced products, used items, or those made from recycled materials. Then pass along what you no longer need for re-use by others.

Adopt these practices for personal purchases and those you make for your business or your workplace.

Look for labels like these on products you buy:

Fair Trade Certified
www.transfairusa.org (U.S.)
www.transfair.ca (Canada)

Forest Stewardship Council
www.fscus.org

International Fairtrade Certification
www.fairtrade.net

Identify vendors who support sustainability through organizations like these:

Sources for socially responsible vendors, pages 18-19

Find used items or recycle what you no longer need through organizations like these:

Craigslist
www.craigslist.org

The Freecycle Network
www.freecycle.org

Goodwill Industries Stores
http://locator.goodwill.org

Nonprofit Recycling and Reuse Network
www.recycles.org

"In the average American's home, there are enough unwanted and unused items to equip a small village. To the owners, these items are clutter that gets in the way of living their lives. But as donations to people who need them, those same items can become a suit to wear to a job interview, or kitchenware for a home of their own. We need to let go, literally, of the baggage of our past and our fear of lack in the future. Do it now, while your discards are still new enough to be of value elsewhere. Find an organization whose mission is in alignment with your values and give your excess baggage a new home."

Breeze Carlile, Piedmont, CA, is a professional coach and move coordinator. She helps relocating clients donate and recycle the clutter in their lives.

6. Reduce your use of non-renewable energy and natural resources.

• •

Conserve resources and replenish what you use.

Climate change is the most significant social issue of our time. Acting to conserve energy and forests is a simple step any coach can take at home and at work. Your actions will influence and inspire your clients, co-workers, and community to do the same.

Take public transit or carpool whenever possible. Explore your options using services like these:

eRideShare
www.erideshare.com

Google Transit
www.google.com/transit

Buy carbon offsets from organizations like these to compensate for home, work, and travel energy use:

Carbonfund
www.carbonfund.org

Terrapass
www.terrapass.com

Use recycled paper products for home, office, and printing from companies like these:

Seventh Generation
www.seventhgeneration.com

Treecycle
www.treecycle.com

Eliminate the use of plastic and polystyrene foam for water bottles, coffee cups, and shopping bags. Carry your own from companies like these:

ChicoBag
www.chicobag.com

Green Home
www.greenhome.com

SIGG Drinking Bottles
www.mysigg.com (U.S.)
www.sigg.com (Canada and U.K.)

"As coaches we are always asking our clients to raise their awareness and be responsible for their results. Naturally, I want to be conscious of my impact on the environment in my daily life and to take responsibility for the state of my city and our planet. I use my energy and influence to care for the environment, standing up for efforts to protect and renew our natural resources and supporting others who do so."

Angela Spaxman, Hong Kong executive coach, is past president of the Int'l Assoc. of Coaching. For two years, she chaired Clear the Air Hong Kong.

7. Eat organic, sustainable, or local food, and low on the food chain.

•••••••••••••••••••••••••••

Change your eating or food-buying habits to protect the environment and your family's health.

Industrial agriculture is one of the largest contributors to environmental degradation worldwide. Consider the facts below, and share them with others who want to increase their positive impact on the planet.

- The global meat industry generates nearly one-fifth of all man-made greenhouse gases.
- 70% of the Amazon rainforest has been lost to livestock pastures and feed crops.
- Conventional agriculture uses antibiotics, synthetic pesticides, and chemical fertilizers on a vast scale, leaving residue in food and polluting water and air.
- 75% of the world's fisheries are either fully exploited, overexploited, or have collapsed.
- A diet made up of local foods consumes up to 17 times less fossil fuel than the typical developed-world diet made up of many foods shipped from far away.

Buy organic or sustainably grown and harvested food. Find out more from:

Organic Consumers Association
www.organicconsumers.org

Seafood Watch
www.seafoodwatch.org

Sustainable Table
www.sustainabletable.org

Find a farmer's market or family farm near you to purchase locally produced foods:

Farmers' Retail & Markets Association (U.K.)
www.farmersmarkets.net

Local Harvest (U.S. and Canada)
www.localharvest.org

Eat less meat, no meat at all, or avoid beef, pork, and lamb. Find out more from:

Go Vegetarian
www.goveg.com

Meatless Monday
www.meatlessmonday.com

> "Coaches are often devoted to helping people with psycho-social challenges. But many of these challenges find their root in a deep alienation from nature. Many of our clients are alienated from their own body, the rhythm of life, experiences of the senses, and connection with other non-human beings. In a global perspective, humans need urgently to reconnect with nature. We all need to care more about our environment, consume less, eat natural food, and take the bike."
>
> *Rudy Vandamme is a coach trainer based in Brussels, Belgium. He is the author of the Dutch bestsellers* **Developmental Coaching Handbook** *and* **The Fork.**

8. Have your business certified as socially responsible or green.

• •

Show your commitment to responsible, sustainable business with a formal certification.

Certifying your business as socially responsible or green sends a message to clients, prospective clients, and your community that you place a priority on responsible, sustainable business. A certification can position you as a leader in social responsibility, make your business more attractive to clients who share your values, and establish a high standard to live up to.

You can obtain a certification for your own business, or encourage your employer to become certified.

Many cities, counties, or regions now have local green business programs. Search the Internet for "green business certification" in your area.

These organizations certify businesses of all types and sizes in socially responsible or green practices in the U.S., Canada, and a growing number of other countries:

B Corporation
www.bcorporation.net

Green America
www.greenamericatoday.org

Green Business Bureau
www.gbb.org

Uniform Standard for Green Biz Certification
www.usgreenbusinesscertification.org

Social responsibility or green certifications are also available for specific industries or products. Find out more from:

Business.gov

www.business.gov/manage/green-business/green-marketing/green-certification.html

Fairtrade Labelling Organizations International

www.fairtrade.net

"I decided to apply for Green America's Seal of Approval after getting involved as a volunteer. I thought I was 'green' before, but the application process asked me to look beyond my own business to those I do business with, to find out how green they are. Their questions aren't just about conservation; they look at labor practices too. So the process creates a ripple effect, and I think that's the point. It's given me a platform for conversations about social issues, and it feels darn good too."

Joan Friedlander coaches entrepreneurs worldwide from Falls Church, VA. Her business is certified by Green America.

9. Do business with socially responsible companies and social enterprises.

• •

Use your personal and business buying power to change the face of business.

Put your money where your values are, and choose to do business with companies who have a strong record of social responsibility. Or seek out social enterprises – organizations who sell products and services with a social mission at their core.

By making your personal and business purchases from socially responsible companies, you encourage businesses everywhere to live up to a higher standard. And when you buy from social enterprises, your money provides funds for a worthy cause.

Find responsible companies from resources like these:

Organizations who certify socially responsible or green companies, page 16

Better World Shopper
www.betterworldshopper.org

Corporate Responsibility Magazine's 100 Best Corporate Citizens
www.thecro.com/content/100-best-corporate-citizens

Find social enterprises from resources like these:

Social Enterprise Alliance (U.S.)
www.se-alliance.org

Social Enterprise Coalition (U.K.)
www.socialenterprise.org.uk

Social Enterprise Marketplace (Canada)
www.secouncil.ca/en/marketplace

Consider doing business with these companies that give a percentage of every purchase to charity:

Better World Books
www.betterworldbooks.com

Give Something Back Business Products
www.givesomethingback.com

GoodShop: The GoodSearch Shopping Mall
www.goodsearch.com/goodshop.aspx

"By doing my shopping only at companies that I know I can believe in, every dollar my family and I spend is a vote of confidence that fuels the types of companies I want to buy from again. If more people acted this way, companies and organizations we can believe in would enjoy an increase in revenue, become more attractive to investors, would hire more people to serve their customers, and create more responsible career choices for us all."

Mrim Boutla, Ph.D., is a career coach and social entrepreneur in Washington, DC. She is co-founder of More than Money Careers.

10. Promote your business with cause marketing.

●●●●●●●●●●●●●●●●●●●●●●●●●●●●●●

Make your marketing budget do double duty by supporting a good cause.

Cause marketing is a vehicle for businesses to support social causes while raising their own visibility. The time and money you spend benefits both the cause and your own enterprise, and makes your business attractive to clients who value social contribution.

Your coaching business can participate in cause marketing, or you can initiate a cause marketing campaign for your employer. Here are some of the many forms that cause marketing can take:

- Launch a public relations campaign to raise money or awareness for a cause you support.
- Become a volunteer spokesperson for a cause, giving talks and interviews, or writing articles about it.
- Donate a percentage of sales to a cause, perhaps from a specific product, service, or program.
- Sponsor or co-sponsor an event – race, auction, dinner, workshop, etc. – that raises funds for a cause.
- Ask your clients to donate to a cause when they do business with you.
- Use your business presence – office area, website, newsletter, exhibit booth, etc. – to promote a cause.
- Partner with a cause to provide them with essential products and services they need.
- Support a cause by providing volunteers. This could be you, your employees or partners, or even clients.

Find out more about cause marketing from resources like these:

Alden Keene's Cause Marketing Blog
www.causerelatedmarketing.blogspot.com

Cause Marketing Forum
www.causemarketingforum.com

Making Money While Making a Difference **by Steckel, Simons, Simons, and Tanen**
www.energizeinc.com/art/amakm.html

Marketing From the Heart **by Peggy Linial**
ww2.causemarketingforum.com/page.asp?ID=189

Olivia Khalili's Cause Capitalism Blog
www.causecapitalism.com

"Investigate cause marketing as part of your overall marketing strategy. When you develop strategic marketing partnerships with nonprofit organizations, you demonstrate your belief in social responsibility and can extend your marketing and sales reach without increasing your budget. Find out what issues are important to your stakeholders, pick one and support it in a big way, and find ways to involve them in your efforts."

Ann Ranson, Dallas, TX, coaches and consults with organizations that want to do well by doing good. As the president of Bottom Line[3] Marketing, she helps her clients hit a "higher note" of impact.

11. Aspire to a high standard of ethics and authenticity.

● ●

You coach others about ethical and authentic behavior; be sure you walk your talk.

Personal integrity is a topic that frequently arises in coaching sessions. We help our clients sort through challenging issues of ethics, integrity, and authenticity. Becoming "squeaky clean" in these areas ourselves gives our coaching more power, and allows us to share helpful examples from our own lives.

Acting with true integrity goes beyond just following rules for ethical behavior. It requires you to be true to yourself, doing what you believe in, and believing in what you do. Speaking and acting in this authentic way inspires trust from your clients and community, and models the behavior you'd most like to see from others.

Find out more about developing personal integrity and authenticity from resources like these:

Finding Your Own North Star **by Martha Beck**
www.marthabeck.com

The Four Agreements **by Don Miguel Ruiz**
www.miguelruiz.com

Leadership and Self-Deception **by Arbinger Institute**
www.arbinger.com

Reclaiming Virtue **by John Bradshaw**
www.johnbradshaw.com

Find out more about ethics and standards for coaches from resources like these:

Assoc. for Coaching Code of Ethics & Good Practice
www.associationforcoaching.com/about/about02.htm

European Mentoring/Coaching Council Ethics Code
www.emccouncil.org/fileadmin/documents/countries/eu
/EMCC_Code_of_Ethics.pdf

International Coach Federation Code of Ethics
www.coachfederation.org/about-icf/ethics/icf-code-of-
ethics/

WABC Code of Business Coaching Ethics/Integrity
http://www.wabccoaches.com/includes/popups/code_of
_ethics_2nd_edition_december_17_2007.html

"Coaching is making a positive impact with clients around the world. However, as more people enter the field, concern continues to be raised about a rapidly growing industry that calls itself a profession, yet remains largely unregulated and unresolved about its agreed-upon knowledge base for competency and professional practice. Therefore, it's critical for coaches to adhere to the highest standards of ethical conduct while demonstrating the values of excellence, integrity, transparency, and respect."

David Matthew Prior is an executive coach on the Columbia coaching faculty based in New York City. For four years he co-chaired the International Coach Federation Ethics and Standards Committee.

12. Stay informed about what's going on around you.

• •

Keep current on problems, solutions, and the efforts of others so you can be an effective change agent.

Changing the world requires some knowledge about what's going on in it. While keeping up with every possible issue would be more than a full-time job, a selective diet of relevant news and information can nourish your changemaking ability.

Below are some options for staying informed about issues that concern you. Choosing just one or two of these will make you a better informed change agent.

- Watch or read the world and national news. Consider CNN, PBS NewsHour, and *The New York Times* (U.S.); CBC News and *The Globe and Mail* (Canada); BBC News and *The Times* (U.K.). For a new perspective, see the news from a country other than your own.
- Read your local metropolitan daily, in print or online.
- Read news and opinion magazines or blogs that cover your areas of interest.
- Listen to podcasts from relevant experts and pundits.
- Learn from thought leaders by reading books and articles they've written or taking classes with them.
- Spend time talking to others who care about the same issues.

Use tools like these to make staying informed easier:

Google Alerts – Receive a daily email about new items on the web for keywords you specify.
www.google.com/alerts

Google Reader – Aggregate blogs and online publications all in one place.
www.google.com/reader/

iTunes – Find and subscribe to podcasts.
www.apple.com/itunes/podcasts/

Slate Magazine's The Slatest – Top news stories of the day, compiled from multiple sources.
http://slatest.slate.com

Twitter – Get instant updates from the thought leaders, media outlets, and institutions you choose.
www.twitter.com

Stay informed about what's going on in coaching:

Coaching publications/social networks, pages 8-9

"We need to be in touch with what's happening in the world because it is a context that gives meaning to coaching. 'Why coaching now?' This is a question we have to keep asking ourselves. Otherwise, it will become out of context and lose its ground in the rapidly changing world. We need to stay awake in order to stay relevant to what's happening and actively participate in its evolution. Coaching has a role to play in keeping all of us awake."

Hide Enomoto, Sagamihara, Japan, introduced career coaching to Japan with his book Coaching. *He is founder of the nonprofit Seven Generations.*

13. Take action on the issues that concern you.

• •

Change starts with you, so start making change.

Changing the world is a pretty big job, and it's easy to get overwhelmed by all the problems to be solved or the many possible ways to help. But instead of waiting to get involved until you figure out the best thing to do, start taking steps to make a difference now.

Once you begin to take action on issues you care about, you'll feel more engaged, meet others on the same path, and discover more about how you can help. Consider some of these options to start making change:

- Become a hands-on volunteer for a cause you care about, if only for a day.
- Donate to a nonprofit that offers sponsorship of a specific person or project you'll receive reports about.
- Join an organization of like-minded people. Attend a meeting or connect online and express your views.
- Talk to your friends and family about problems that concern you and advocate for solutions you support.
- Use your social media network to promote a cause.
- Post comments on news stories, write letters to editors, or compose an op-ed sharing your opinions.
- Write letters or make calls to political leaders or corporate executives requesting action on an issue.
- Call in to radio and TV shows when issues that concern you are being discussed.
- Support political candidates who share your views by volunteering for or donating to campaigns.
- Research election issues and vote your conscience.

The following resources can help you take action:

Better World Handbook's Amazing Organizations
www.betterworldhandbook.com/action10(orgs).html

Citizen You **by Jonathan Tisch and Karl Weber**
www.citizenyou.org

Giving **by Bill Clinton**
http://giving.clintonfoundation.org

NPAction's Tips for Letters to Editors and Op-Eds
www.npaction.org/article/articleview/618/1/229

Project VoteSmart
www.votesmart.org

Soul of a Citizen **by Paul Rogat Loeb**
www.paulloeb.org

"We all have family, work, financial, and practical life issues to deal with and wonder how it might be possible to get beyond where we are now to something that feels more significant and fulfilling. It doesn't have to be a scary jump off a cliff. It simply means taking first steps to explore what and how, design a plan, and keep moving from there. It's amazing where that can go."

Dolly Garlo coaches on careers and business from Key West, FL. Through CreatingLegacy.com she helps people make lasting personal contributions.

14. Overcome the fear, resistance, or self-sabotage that holds you back.

●●●●●●●●●●●●●●●●●●●●●●●●●●●●●

To change the world, you may first need to change yourself.

What is it that prevents you from making the difference you know you could? Are you fearful of taking risks or of what people might think? Are you resistant to changing old habits or entering new territory? Do patterns of self-sabotage repeatedly stop you?

Negative beliefs and unproductive habits don't just hold back your own success; they hinder your ability to do more good in the world. To be of maximum service to others, strive to remove your own limitations.

Consider some of these approaches to breaking through fear, resistance, and self-sabotage:

- Work on these issues with your own coach. Set a coaching agenda that makes this work a priority.
- Participate in a support group, success team, or mastermind group where you can work with others on removing barriers to positive change.
- Read some of the books listed below and work with the exercises they provide. Most of these authors also offer workshops or groups to help.
- Engage in a spiritual practice, meditation, or a martial art that helps you to find your center and overcome self-defeating beliefs and behavior.

The following resources offer helpful tools:

Feel the Fear and Do It Anyway **by Susan Jeffers**
www.susanjeffers.com

Fearless Living by **Rhonda Britten**
www.fearlessliving.com

First Things First by **Stephen R. Covey**
www.stephencovey.com

Making a Change for Good by **Cheri Huber**
www.cherihuber.com

Taking the Leap: Freeing Ourselves from Old Habits and Fears by **Pema Chodron**
www.shambhala.org/teachers/pema/

Taming Your Gremlin by **Rick Carson**
www.tamingyourgremlin.com

What Got You Here Won't Get You There by **Marshall Goldsmith**
www.marshallgoldsmithlibrary.com

"The vast majority of people, no matter how confident they appear to be, harbor paralyzing fears that lurk beneath the surface. These inner demons are always at the ready to whisper skeptical objections and plant doubts about anything that might shake up the status quo. There is no 'right' time to begin living fearlessly. Wherever you are is the perfect place to start."

Rhonda Britten is an Emmy Award-winning life coach based in Los Angeles who has changed lives in over 600 episodes of reality TV, and authored four books including her groundbreaking **Fearless Living.**

PART II:
CHANGE THE WORLD
WITH YOUR COACHING

You probably spend more of your life working in your business or job than at any other single activity except sleeping. With so much of your time, energy, and focus devoted to your primary career, it is here that you can have the most impact on the world.

As a coach, you may have more opportunities than most to dedicate your professional time to world-changing pursuits. You can make positive change your full-time vocation, or design your business or job to include a focus on changemaking.

Either way, making intentional choices about how you coach, who you coach, and where you coach will significantly increase your contribution to making the world a better place.

15. Design your coaching practice to serve your highest purpose.

● ●

Choose who, where, and how you will coach to reflect your life purpose and honor your gifts.

When you begin practicing as a coach, whether you choose self-employment or a salaried job, you are at choice. You can choose to coach any client who shows up or select those you want, to engage in activities that serve an end or those that fulfill you, to focus on making the most money or on making the most difference.

Consider these ways to consciously design a coaching practice that aligns with your life purpose:

- Choose a coaching niche that allows you to work with clients you feel called to serve.
- Design your business or career to make maximum use of your gifts and avoid what drags you down.
- Create personal standards and boundaries that govern who, where, and how you coach.
- Surround yourself with colleagues who support your purpose and respect your gifts.
- Incorporate into your coaching the themes, tools, and practices that best reflect who you truly are.

Articles about serving a higher purpose with coaching:

"Coaching to Change the World" by C.J. Hayden
www.cjhayden.com/social-change/coaching-change/

"Give from Your Heart and Change the World" by Virginia Kellogg and Beth Wallace
www.leadershipthatworks.com/documentFiles/154.pdf

"The Difference You Want to Make as a Life Coach" by Jason Westlake
www.jasonwestlake.com/the-difference-you-want-to-make-as-a-life-coach/

Books on how to identify your life purpose and incorporate it in your work:

The Power of Purpose by Richard Leider
www.richardleider.com

A New Earth: Awakening to Your Life's Purpose by Eckhart Tolle
www.eckharttolle.com

To Build the Life You Want, Create the Work You Love by Marsha Sinetar
www.marshasinetar.com

"When I first began coaching, I coached anyone who would hire me. I was hesitant to limit my opportunities by defining a specialty. But I found purpose in working with clients who were courageous enough to be authentic. Over the years I've refined this niche. I now work with those who consciously choose to live what I call their Active Legacy®, created moment-by-moment through choices and actions according to their values and beliefs."

Vikki Brock, Ph.D., coaches leaders internationally from her 50' trimaran in Ventura, CA. She is the author of Sourcebook of Coaching History.

16. Commit to "first, do no harm" with your coaching.

• •

Determine what you will and won't support with your coaching in order to serve the greatest good.

A basic precept of medical ethics is to "first, do no harm." It reminds doctors that some interventions can have unintended consequences which, on the whole, do more harm than good.

When you coach a person or organization that is engaged in activities you believe are unethical or socially irresponsible, are you helping the world or harming it? Would you continue to coach a client who reveals they are participating in abuse, fraud, or neglect? When might you be able to change a situation by continuing to coach those involved, and when might your continued support enable behavior to which you are morally opposed?

Only you can decide where your personal boundaries lie, but here are some areas to consider:

• What industries or professions would you be unwilling to work for as a coach?

• What constitutes harmful or unethical behavior in your view? What "red flags" might alert you to it?

• What action would you take if a client reveals unethical behavior? Or if you learn about it elsewhere? And if that behavior persists?

• How would you coach a client around their own ethical conflicts with activities they participate in?

The following resources can help you determine the boundaries between doing good and causing harm:

"Buddhist Ethics for a Harm-Free Livelihood" by Josh Schrei

www.huffingtonpost.com/josh-schrei/a-livelihood-that-does-no_b_591612.html

Law and Ethics in Coaching **by Patrick Williams and Sharon K. Anderson**

www.lifecoachtraining.com

"Leadership: Facing Moral and Ethical Dilemmas" by David Lassiter

www.exe-coach.com/moralAndEthicalDilemmas.html

The MBA Oath

www.mbaoath.org

"For me, 'first, do no harm' means thinking about the world as an interconnected system. I am part of that system. When I put my energy into clients, organizations, or anything else, I want to improve society, people, and the planet. And I don't want to add to or support the things I perceive as harmful. In addition, this principle means not doing harm to my clients. I am careful about boundaries, intentions, and expectations."

Beth Shapiro, Boston, MA, coaches leaders, teams, and whole organizations. She serves on the faculty of two coaching schools and has a master's in public administration from Harvard's Kennedy School.

17. Coach your clients about social responsibility.

• •

Take a stand for social responsibility with your clients, just as you would for life balance or self-care.

Social responsibility is the ethical principle which holds that individuals and organizations have a responsibility to the society in which they exist. The emerging view of social responsibility goes beyond simply doing no harm; it requires giving back. When people or organizations benefit from society, social responsibility indicates they should reciprocate.

Introducing social responsibility into your coaching may seem as if you are intruding your own agenda. But in reality, coaches *do* have an agenda for their clients.

When you notice that clients are ignoring their work/life balance, you call it to their attention. If a client said he or she was doing something illegal, you would speak up. If you see clients harming themselves through substance abuse or ignoring their health, you address it. Why, then, would social responsibility be a taboo topic?

Consider these possibilities for bringing social responsibility into your coaching sessions:

- Ask your clients what values they hold about social responsibility and how they might like to address these during coaching.
- Notice when clients express concerns related to social responsibility and name what you see.
- Suggest social responsibility as an agenda item when coaching in organizations, or designing team coaching and strategic planning sessions.

The following resources suggest ways to address social responsibility with your clients:

"The Challenge of Global Leadership"
Keynote Address by Sir John Whitmore
www.youtube.com/watch?v=7-D6CnaQUuw

"Coaching for Sustainability"
Case Study Series by Article 13 Group
www.article13.com/csr/sustainability_coaching.asp

"Going Green: Coaching for Social Responsibility"
Podcast from Insight Educational Consulting
www.ieconsulting.biz/index.aspx?urlname=going-green-coaching-for-social-responsibility

"I increasingly find that issues of social responsibility have become material to many of the executives I coach. What was once considered peripheral is now central as businesses deal with dwindling resources, increasing commodity prices, and the difficulty of recruiting talent. This is a conversation that coaches need to be having, as it sets the macro context within which many of our clients are operating. They face change and complexity on an unprecedented scale. Are they able as leaders to step up into this complexity and be systemic in their decision making?"

Neela Bettridge is a leadership coach and sustainability advisor in London, England. She is a founding partner of the CSR firm Article 13 and authors the sustainability blog Radical Shift.

18. Coach youth, especially those at risk.

●●●●●●●●●●●●●●●●●●●●●●●●●●●●●

Coach the next generation and you'll empower them to build a better world for us all.

Imagine how different your life might have been if you had received coaching as a child or teenager. Coaching unlocks our potential to achieve great deeds, solve life's problems, and build a fulfilling future. Coaching young people enables them to tap into that potential at an early age, empowering them to potentially become world-changers themselves.

Young people who experience coaching typically raise their self-esteem, gain confidence in their abilities, and become more resilient to stress. These positive qualities give them the strength and ability to help not only themselves, but their friends, family, and community to lead more enriching lives.

Almost any young person could benefit from coaching, but for disadvantaged youth in particular, coaching can play a key role in improving their prospects. Coaching can help at-risk young people stay in school, increase their leadership abilities, and make smarter choices about their future.

Here are some possible avenues for coaching youth:

- Volunteer to coach young people in your community or through a national organization.
- Target youth or families as clients for your paid coaching services.
- Train young people in coaching skills so they can become peer coaches for each other.
- Train parents or teachers in coaching skills so they can coach the young people in their world.

These resources will help you learn more about coaching youth:

Coaching 4 Teens
www.coaching4teens.org

Coaching Kids
www.coachingkids.org

"Creating a Better Future" by Randy Nathan
www.projectnextgen.com/choicearticle.pdf

"Study Reveals Coaches Can Have Success Coaching Kids" by Mark Joyella
www.coachingcommons.org/featured/coaching-research-study-reveals-coaches-can-have-success-coaching-kids-to-better-performance/

"When Coaching Kids brought life coaching skills to a group of incarcerated young girls, the transformation we witnessed was remarkable. They discovered new ways to view themselves and the world, a vision of a positive future, and an opportunity for real change. They learned that failing is part of the process of life and that staying the course and recovering are keys to attaining success. Young people have an immense ability to change, and coaching has the power to make that happen."

Reuel J. Hunt is a leadership coach in Highlands Ranch, CO. He is the founder of the nonprofit Coaching Kids.

19. Coach people who face racial and ethnic discrimination.

● ●

Help overcome discrimination and disadvantage by coaching those who experience it.

Members of minority groups are considerably less likely to receive coaching than are the majority groups in their country. When most coaches in a given country are from the majority, their clients are most often other majority group members. And with coaching more available to those with higher incomes, minorities – typically with lower incomes overall – can be excluded.

But when people from minority groups do work with a coach, they often find their coach's support invaluable in overcoming bias and discrimination on the job, in school, and in their community. Coaching helps them to succeed in challenging environments, improving their economic status, and increasing their ability to make valuable contributions to the world as a whole.

If you are from a minority group yourself, you might choose to coach other minority group members as your entire coaching niche or a designated portion of it.

Regardless of your own status, strive to serve a more diverse population. Reach out to minority communities in your marketing and networking. Study resources like those below to become more comfortable with coaching the unique issues that minority clients may raise.

Recognize also that as more minority group members receive coaching, it's likely that more will become coaches. That shift will begin to make coaching more accessible to all.

These resources will tell you more about coaching minority group members:

The CCL Handbook of Coaching: **"Coaching Leaders of Color" by Ancella B. Livers**
www.ccl.org

Coaching Across Cultures **by Philippe Rosinski**
www.philrosinski.com

"Coaching Across Differences" by Martha Lasley
www.nvccoach.org/2010/03/coaching-across-differences.html

Diversity in Coaching **edited by Jonathan Passmore**
www.associationforcoaching.com/home/acbookstore.htm

"I pioneered culturally competent coaching, because I believe that cultural identity and beliefs generate behavior patterns that can be subconsciously destructive, and invisible. This is called 'internalized oppression.' To continuously fall into the cultural hypnosis of thinking that the dominant culture controls anyone's lives is a true abdication of personal power. Coaching, especially at the level of cultural identity, can create massive 'internalized freedom,' and who doesn't want that?"

Veronica Conway, Sausalito, CA, is a coach and facilitator. She founded the Black Professional Coaches Alliance, authored "The Black Paper" and created the Black Mastery Success Program.

20. Coach people with disabilities.

••••••••••••••••••••••••••••••

Coach individuals with disabilities to make the most of their talents and skills.

People with mental and physical disabilities and chronic illness are frequently excluded from participating as valued members of their community. They may experience discrimination, limited opportunities, or lack of acceptance by others.

With coaching, people with disabilities and chronic illness can boost their self-esteem, become more assertive about their rights to equal treatment or accommodation, and improve their employment prospects. Career coaching, job coaching, and life skills coaching can enable people with disabilities to not only better support themselves, but contribute more to their communities.

Job coaching is a recognized specialty in employment development, and does not have to involve assessment or counseling. The job coach's primary function is often to coach people with disabilities in learning the requirements of a specific job and improving their interpersonal skills.

Consider these ways to coach people with disabilities:

- Volunteer to coach people with disabilities in your area, or virtually through a national organization.
- Include people with disabilities or chronic illness as clients you target for your paid coaching services.
- Seek employment as a job coach or life skills coach with a government agency or nonprofit that serves individuals with disabilities.
- Train people with disabilities in coaching skills so they can serve as peer coaches for each other.

Learn more about coaching people with disabilities from these resources:

"Career Coaching and Disability" by Monica J. Foster
www.butterflywheel.com/archives/787

"Chronic Illness Coaching Shows Significant Benefits" by Jason Reid
www.sickwithsuccess.com/study-help/

"A Coach's Creed: Balancing Work and Life for the Chronically Ill" by Amy Tenderich
www.diatribe.us/issues/5/profile.php

VCU Rehabilitation Research and Training Center
www.worksupport.com

YWCA Life Skills Coach Training & Manuals
www.ywcatoronto.org/lifeskills_training

"Life can be overwhelming at times for people with disabilities. But just 'getting through the day' isn't enough. We were all put on this earth for a purpose, and the sooner we can put our unique talents to work, the sooner we can realize our true potential. Working with a coach can help people with disabilities shift their thinking from frustration to hope, from dread to anticipation, and from hopelessness to hopefulness about the incredible future that lies ahead."

Monica J. Foster, Landis, NC, coaches people with disabilities and chronic illnesses. She was born with spina bifida and uses a wheelchair.

21. Coach in the developing world.

● ●

Use the tools of coaching to help people in developing countries help themselves.

Throughout the developing world, resources are limited. Communities and their leaders are focused on the basic needs for survival – food, clean water, shelter, health care, and safety. The support of a coach can help people who are struggling to survive build a vision of a brighter future and discover new solutions for the challenges they face.

Developing world coaches assist community leaders with problem-solving, strategic thinking, managing priorities, and self-development, aiding them to uplift their communities. Coaches also help the citizens of developing countries navigate challenges with work, business, money, health care, parenting, communicating, and relationships.

Here are some options for bringing coaching to the developing world:

- Provide coaching to leaders, entrepreneurs, teachers, and other influencers located in developing countries through a local or international non-governmental organization (NGO).
- Coach the next generation of developing world leaders to help initiate a coaching culture in their communities.
- Coach the leaders and staff of NGOs and other visionaries who are working to resolve developing world problems.
- Train developing world community leaders, educators, caregivers, and motivated citizens in coaching skills so they can coach others.
- Develop coaching tools and approaches that can be employed affordably in developing world communities.

These resources will tell you more about coaching in the developing world:

The Brande Foundation Coaching Project
www.thecoachingproject.org

Coaching the Global Village
www.coachingtheglobalvillage.org

Leadership Beyond Boundaries
www.leadbeyond.org

NGO Use of Coaching Interventions **by Lynne Gilliland and Robert A. Jud**
www.gillilandjud.com/pdfs/NGO_Coaching_Booklet.pdf

"The 'coach approach' can empower local and rural communities within developing world countries to be more resourceful. The NGOs that supply food, water, housing, etc., can also benefit from a holistic coaching approach in order to create and empower sustainable changes. Taking this global and integrative perspective for the power of coaching, we can do much for the view that coaching is mostly elitist and primarily serves the rich and powerful."

Patrick Williams, Ed.D., Palm Coast, FL, is the founder of the Institute for Life Coach Training and author of five books on coaching. He founded the nonprofit Coaching the Global Village.

22. Coach in the nonprofit sector.

• •

Coach the leaders and staff of nonprofits to increase organizational effectiveness and job performance.

The adoption of coaching in the nonprofit sector lags behind its widespread use in the corporate world. But when nonprofits do make use of coaches, they develop more effective leaders and staff, building the capacity of their organizations to carry out their mission.

Nonprofit leaders who receive coaching improve their ability to think strategically, solve problems, manage with confidence and integrity, and make conscious decisions for their organizations.

Staff at all levels who work with a coach raise their awareness about how their behavior impacts others, become better at prioritizing and delegating, and will typically both increase their job satisfaction and improve their performance.

Coaching can have a ripple effect in nonprofits, where coaching leaders improves their ability to lead, strengthening the entire organization, and therefore spreading its impact to the communities being served.

Consider these options for coaching nonprofits:

- Volunteer to coach nonprofit leaders or staff for a local nonprofit or through a national organization.
- Target nonprofits as clients for your paid coaching services.
- Seek employment as a coach with a company or support organization that serves nonprofits.
- Train nonprofit staff in coaching skills so they can serve as internal coaches for their organizations.

Learn more about coaching in the nonprofit sector from these resources:

The Coach Approach
www.coachapproachinc.org

The Coach Initiative
www.coachinitiative.org

Coaching and Philanthropy Project Toolkit
https://groups.compasspoint.org/coachingnonprofits/

Coaching Skills for Nonprofit Managers and Leaders
by Judith Wilson and Michelle Gislason
www.compasspoint.org/coachingbook

The Power of Coaching (in Nonprofits)
www.haasjr.org/programs-and-initiatives/video/power-coaching

"A nonprofit executive called and said, 'How do I tell my staff we have to shut down because we have no money?' I started to ask questions. I could hear the hope in her voice as she replied. That hope generated new creative solutions. Coaching multiplied her success with the people her organization serves. 85% of them never go back to an abusive situation again. That's changing the world."

Carlo Jensen, Calgary, Canada, coaches leaders who care. He is the former Director of Consulting at CentrePoint Nonprofit Management and has worked with over 600 nonprofits.

23. Coach political leaders and people in government.

●●●●●●●●●●●●●●●●●●●●●●●●●●●●●●

Encourage vision, focus, and integrity in government and politics by coaching leaders and staff.

Imagine a world where political and government leaders evaluate each strategy and decision with their coach before making a move, considering carefully how their choices fit into their vision, honor their values, and allow them to achieve their long-range goals. Now compare that to how you see most of these decisions being made now.

The arenas of politics and government could clearly benefit from increased attention to integrity, values, and long-range vision, and these are some of the many benefits that working with a coach can bring.

Here are some possibilities for coaching in politics and government:

- Coach elected officials and candidates for public office, including during their campaigns.
- Coach managers and staff in local, regional, and national government departments.
- Provide coaching to the members of boards and councils who influence government policies.
- Coach the campaign managers, political consultants, party leaders, organizers, and lobbyists who set standards for political behavior.
- Provide team coaching for government agencies.
- Train government leaders and staff in coaching skills so they can coach others in their arena.

The following resources offer perspectives and tools for coaching political leaders and people in government:

"Coaching in Government" by Donna Karlin

www.abetterperspective.com/IJCO612008Karlin52_68fin aureprint.pdf

Leadership Coaching: "Chapter 7 - Coaching Political Leaders" by Jean Hartley and Kate Pinder

www.associationforcoaching.com/home/book4.htm

"Consider Hiring a Political Coach" by Donna Zajonc

www.winningcampaigns.org/Winning-Campaigns-Archive-Articles/Hire-a-Political-Coach.html

"Working within government is enriching, energizing and rewarding. Every day brings an awareness of the workings of the government, our governing party, Canadian policies, our impact on the world, and our place in the world as a whole. Coaching leaders in government gives me a sense of making a difference while, at the same time, validating my role as a coach. I help clients bridge the gap between where they currently are and where they want to be, and how that translates to better serving Canada and its people."

Donna Karlin, Ottawa, Canada, coaches global executives and political leaders. She pioneered the practice of Shadow Coaching® with organizational leaders in the public and private sectors.

24. Coach activists and advocates for social change.

● ●

Change the world by coaching those who are working to change it.

Being an activist is a way of life rather than one single profession. Advocates for social change can be found in many positions and occupations, leading, organizing, educating, motivating, and inspiring others.

When you reach out as a coach with the message that you support social change, you can attract and serve clients who share that aim, regardless of how they are working to accomplish it.

Here are some of the many varieties of activists you might choose to support with your coaching:

- Leaders, including those in business, nonprofits, government, churches, and the community
- Organizers, including those engaged in outreach, advocacy, lobbying, or direct action
- Volunteers who serve social change causes
- Philanthropists who fund social missions
- Educators, including teachers, professors, workshop leaders, and lecturers
- Journalists, including reporters, editors, columnists, bloggers, and broadcast personalities
- Writers, including authors, feature writers, novelists, playwrights, songwriters, and poets
- Performers, including actors, singers, dancers, and performance artists
- Artists, including painters, muralists, sculptors, photographers, and filmmakers

Learn more about coaching in the social change arena from these resources:

Coach for Peace
www.coachforpeace.org/mission

Coaching for Social Change
http://sites.google.com/site/coachingforsocialchange/

Firedoglake Book Salon on *The Lifelong Activist*
Interview with Hillary Rettig
http://fdl.me/bGyPI5

Mirus Coaching for Social Change
www.miruscoaching.org

"Activism is a glorious life with many rewards, but it also has challenges. Constantly bucking the status quo can be wearying, as can focusing on the world's inequalities and cruelties. Activism tends to be badly paid, when it is paid at all. All of this can easily lead to stress and burnout. Activists must invest in a lot of self-care and support. I love coaching and otherwise supporting activists because they tend to be wonderful people who are doing important work. And I love that by helping activists become happier and more effective, I am helping heal society as a whole."

Hillary Rettig, Boston, MA, is a coach and activist who helps ambitious, creative people overcome what holds them back. She is the author of **The Lifelong Activist** *and* **The 7 Secrets of the Prolific.**

25. Coach conscious capitalists.

●●●●●●●●●●●●●●●●●●●●●●●●●●●●●

Coach the leaders who are reshaping business as a force for social good.

There's a growing movement around the world to make use of business and the tools of capitalism as a force for good. CEOs, entrepreneurs, and executives are increasingly insisting that their businesses must serve a "triple bottom line," contributing to people and the planet, not just to profit.

Coaching these conscious business leaders can assist them in achieving ambitious goals, staying true to their vision, honoring their values, withstanding criticism, and building an organizational culture that will keep their vision and values intact.

Conscious capitalists and the enterprises they direct go by many different names. To seek out people like this to coach, look for socially responsible business, conscious business, triple bottom line business, not-just-for-profit business, green business, sustainable business, social sector business, B Corporations, community interest companies (CICs), low-profit limited liability companies (L3Cs), social benefit corporations, social enterprises, social ventures, or social entrepreneurs.

Find out more about conscious capitalism and triple bottom line business from these resources:

Be the Solution: How Entrepreneurs and Conscious Capitalists Can Solve All the World's Problems **by Michael Strong**
www.flowidealism.org

B Corporation
www.bcorporation.net

Business Alliance for Local Living Economies
www.livingeconomies.org

Conscious Capitalism Institute
www.consciouscapitalism.org

Conscious Leader Network
www.consciousleadernetwork.com

Firms of Endearment **by Rajendra S. Sisodia, et al.**
www.firmsofendearment.com

Triple Pundit
www.triplepundit.com

"Traditional capitalism puts profit and shareholders at the forefront, whilst conscious business values all stakeholders equally: employees, suppliers, partners, customers, shareholders, society, and the environment. Conscious business has a greater purpose than simply to make a profit. Conscious leaders don't allow one group to benefit at the expense of another. It's not a zero-sum game. I don't have to lose out if you win, and you don't have to lose out if I win. If you win, I win too. How refreshing is that for business?"

Gina Hayden coaches conscious leaders globally from her base in London, England. She heads up The Conscious Leadership Consultancy and co-founded the Global Institute for Conscious Leadership.

26. Coach social entrepreneurs.

● ●

Support the innovators whose ideas for wide-scale change could transform the world.

Social entrepreneurs are leaders who employ entrepreneurial principles to create positive social change. They launch innovative, pattern-breaking ventures in either the nonprofit or for-profit sector, and create replicable systems that they or others can use to expand the impact of their ideas.

Just as a business entrepreneur transforms an idea into an enterprise, a social entrepreneur invents a new approach for solving a problem in society and implements it on a wide scale, by building an organization, network, or even a movement.

When you coach social entrepreneurs, you help these changemakers maximize their potential to envision, introduce, and advance their revolutionary innovations.

Here are some approaches for coaching social entrepreneurs:

- Target social entrepreneurs as clients for your paid coaching services.
- Volunteer to coach social entrepreneurs through an organization that supports them.
- Seek employment as a coach with a support organization that serves social entrepreneurs.
- Train support organization staff in coaching skills so they can provide coaching to those they serve.

Find out more about social entrepreneurs and possibilities for coaching them from these resources:

Ashoka
www.ashoka.org

The Brande Foundation Coaching Project
www.thecoachingproject.org

"Coaching Social Entrepreneurs" by C.J. Hayden
www.socialentrepreneurcoach.com/resources/coaching-social-entrepreneurs.html

The Tactics of Hope: How Social Entrepreneurs Are Changing Our World **by Wilford Welch & David Hopkins**
www.tacticsofhope.org

Social Edge
www.socialedge.org

"Traditional leadership programs typically focus on what the leader does or what the leader can get others to do… The focus in life coaching is on what leaders can be, on how leaders can improve themselves such that the people around them are more likely to be effective in a more natural way. When I think of the best leaders… I think of people who drew others to them because they were so clear in their own hearts where they were headed that folks wanted to go there with them."

Dave Ellis, Marin County, CA, founded the Brande Foundation to provide pro bono coaching to social entrepreneurs and nonprofits. He donates all profits from his company to the foundation.

27. Offer group or team coaching to impact more clients.

• •

Leverage the power of groups and teams to make coaching more affordable and accessible.

Coaching people in groups allows you to make more impact with your coaching in several ways:
- Each participant can pay a lower price to receive coaching, making it more affordable for all.
- You increase your capacity to provide coaching by working with multiple people at once.
- Group or team coaching is often more attractive to companies and organizations than one-on-one work, allowing new entry points for coaching.
- Team coaching can have a long-lasting positive impact on the overall effectiveness of a group.
- Participants in groups often become peer coaches for each other, and bring this approach back to their workplace or community.
- Coaching groups may provide you with a higher income, freeing up time for other service work.

There are many ways to provide group coaching:
- Offer coaching groups to the public, focused on specific audiences and/or themes.
- Form a coaching group made up of specific individuals you already know.
- Offer group coaching or team coaching to companies, organizations, and institutions for their staff, members, or students.
- Provide a group coaching program for clients of a nonprofit, community center, or social agency.

Learn more about coaching groups from these resources:

33 Minute Mastery: Group Coaching in 33 Minutes
Home-Study Course by Wendy Y. Bailey
www.groupcoachingmastery.com

Group Coaching: A Comprehensive Blueprint
by Ginger Cockerham
www.coachginger.com

Effective Group Coaching **by Jennifer J. Britton**
www.groupcoachingessentials.com

Group and Team Coaching **by Christine Thornton**
www.thorntonconsulting.org

"There is real power and passion in creating a group coaching environment. …each member commits to take the actions necessary to reach their goals and complete their mission. In the process, they tap into the collective energy, experience, and wisdom that are held within the group. As a result, the individuals are encouraged and inspired to commit to moving forward, then to take the action steps they have identified as necessary to achieve their goals, and to excel in the supportive environment of a coaching group."

Ginger Cockerham, Dallas, TX, is a business and life coach who has been coaching groups in companies and organizations since 1997.

28. Educate the public about coaching as a tool for change.

● ●

Spread the word about the power of coaching to accelerate change.

One of the barriers to creating positive change in the world is the difficult nature of change itself. Change brings up fear, resistance, doubt, and feelings of inadequacy. It takes a strong leader to keep people moving forward in changing times. And individuals need a solid framework of life skills to navigate change successfully. Coaching can provide exactly the support leaders and individuals need to be better changemakers.

Approaches you can use to educate the public about coaching as a change tool include:
- Writing articles, case studies, or white papers
- Writing blog posts or guest blogging for others
- Speaking for local and national organizations
- Speaking on podcasts, teleseminars, and webinars
- Giving interviews for print and broadcast media

You can gather research data from resources like these:

International Coach Federation Research Portal
www.coachfederation.org/research-education/

Coaching and Philanthropy Project Toolkit
https://groups.compasspoint.org/coachingnonprofits/

Sherpa Coaching Resource Center
www.sherpacoaching.com/executive-coaching-research.html

These resources will help you be more effective at getting the word out:

Coaches Make a Difference PR Toolkit

www.coachesmakeadifference.org/free-resources/

Get Slightly Famous **by Steven Van Yoder**

www.getslightlyfamous.com

Sell Yourself without Selling Your Soul **by Susan Harrow**

www.prsecrets.com

Writing to Make a Difference **by Dalya F. Massachi**

www.dfmassachi.net

"I am really pleased that so many coaches have participated in International Coaching Week. It is very gratifying to know that so many people are offering pro bono coaching and other community events in such a heartfelt way. When I started this in 1999, I had no idea that it would soon take on a life of its own. I really am delighted that this Week is becoming a focal point for both publicizing coaching worldwide and providing the public with a sense of the possibilities that coaching offers."

Jerri Udelson, Santa Fe, NM, coaches entrepreneurs and professionals. She founded International Coaching Week to promote the profession of coaching.

29. Learn more about changemaking to serve your clients as a resource.
● ●
You'll be a better guide if you know the territory.

It's possible to coach effectively when a client's area of endeavor is unfamiliar to you. But learning more about the kind of changemaking you'd like to support with coaching can increase your capacity to serve:

- Speaking the same language as your clients can be a shortcut to understanding their goals and plans.
- Suggesting role models or business models to clients can aid them in designing their own path.
- Becoming aware of organizations, communities, periodicals, and influential people in your chosen field will assist you in marketing yourself.

Consider these approaches to becoming better acquainted with any changemaking field you choose:

- Look up topics in Google or the Wikipedia
- Read books and magazines – Google them, find them on Amazon, or visit a bookstore
- Search for videos on YouTube
- Follow columns, blogs, newsletters, and podcasts
- Participate in online communities
- Attend association meetings, conferences, and networking meetups
- Take classes and workshops
- Earn a certificate, credential, or degree
- Interview experts and centers of influence

The following resources can help you learn more about any topic or field:

Google Scholar
http://scholar.google.com

Research Strategies **by William Badke**
www.acts.twu.ca/Library/textbook.htm

RefDesk Online News & Reference Index
www.refdesk.com

Technorati Blog Index
www.technorati.com

WorldCat Library Catalog
www.worldcat.org

Weddle's Association Directory
www.weddles.com/associations/index.cfm

"The more I learn about my clients' industry and organizational context, the better I am able to coach and support them in their change-making work. In addition to academic studies in my clients' field, I have actively sought out blogs, podcasts, news websites, social media networks, and industry thought leaders on Twitter. As a result, my clients instantly feel that I get where they're coming from, and my coaching is more effective."

Shana Montesol Johnson coaches aid and international development professionals worldwide from Manila, Philippines. She earned a master's in international development at Harvard's Kennedy School.

30. Champion the world-changing goals of your clients.

• •

Call forth the greatness your clients need to change the world.

Clients engaged in changemaking can experience more than the usual number of critics and naysayers. Well-meaning advisors will tell them their vision is too big or their dream is impossible. Skeptics will say they'll never make a living at world-changing, and they ought to give up and get a real job. Since many people will tell your clients "you can't do that," what clients need to hear from you instead is, "how *can* you do that?"

Championing, acknowledgement, challenging, and calling forth are key skills for coaching changemakers. Especially in the early stages of a changemaking venture, you may be the one positive voice they hear that can help them keep going. And that may require suspending some of your own disbelief about what is and isn't possible. Your vision of possibility needs to be as big – or bigger – than that of your clients.

Learn to challenge and champion your clients toward building their vision of change. Ask them tough questions that spur them beyond their comfort zone. Challenge them to talk to important people and ask for help they may not believe they can get. Acknowledge their ability to do things they've never done before. Hold up the mirror and show them the world-changing vision they shared with you, and let them know you believe in it too. Call forth their greatness.

Learn more about calling forth your clients' greatness from these resources:

Coaching into Greatness by **Kim George**
www.coachingintogreatness.com

Coachville Learning Guide: "Elicits Greatness"
www.coachville.com/public/download/?file_id=4451708

**"Forward the Action, Deepen the Learning"
by Corrina Gordon-Barnes, CPCC**
www.thecoaches.com/resources/multimedia/Co-Active-
Contexts-Deepen-The-Learning.html

Resources for overcoming fear, resistance, and self-sabotage, page 29

> "Championing the world-changing goals of my clients is why I am a coach. It is my calling. Everyone has a role to play in the evolution and healing of our planetary Self and the heart is yearning to fulfill its highest destiny. The only things that can prevent clients from changing the world are their own limiting thoughts. Coaching that calls forth a client's full potential can be a key to unlocking this great purpose."
>
> *Ryan Eliason, Eugene, OR, coaches business owners and social entrepreneurs. He founded the international nonprofit YES! at the age of 19.*

31. Make use of coaching skills in all spheres of your life.

• •

Employing the coach approach can facilitate change in any arena.

Engaging in coaching conversations can help people gain clarity, shift perspectives, focus on what's important, broaden their vision, and align with others around a shared purpose. Clearly, conversations like these could benefit any individual or group interested in causing change.

Coaching skills can have applications far beyond their use within a formal coaching relationship. Using skills such as powerful questions, reflective listening, requesting, and accountability can boost your effectiveness in situations such as:

- Supporting people and groups to expand their vision and achieve their goals
- Helping individuals learn new skills and attitudes that will aid their success at changemaking
- Introducing new perspectives on issues to friends, family, and colleagues
- Leading a team of volunteers, employees, or collaborators
- Facilitating meetings with stakeholders from different camps
- Interacting with community leaders, government officials, and corporate representatives
- Asking for behavior or policy changes from individuals and institutions

These resources will tell you more about using a coaching approach in everyday life:

Co-Active Coaching **by Laura Whitworth, Karen and Henry Kimsey-House, and Phillip Sandahl**

www.thecoaches.com/resources/books/books-on-coaching.html

Coaching for Performance: GROWing Human Potential and Purpose **by John Whitmore**

www.performanceconsultants.com/header-coaching

Creating Leaderful Organizations: **How to Bring Out Leadership in Everyone by Joseph A. Raelin**

www.northeastern.edu/poe/about/bookpage.html

Turning to One Another **by Margaret J. Wheatley**

www.margaretwheatley.com

"Although I am a fervent advocate of professional coaching, I feel that the greatest application of coaching comes in everyday living. It is in our relationships with our co-workers, family, children, and friends that we can fully utilize and practice coaching. Coaching is an approach to be more effective and in better relationship with those people that matter most."

Karen Kimsey-House is the co-founder of The Coaches Training Institute in San Rafael, CA, and the co-author of **Co-Active Coaching**.

32. Hold the entire world as your client.

● ●

Broaden your concept of who and what your coaching serves.

Our traditional view of coaching is that we coach one person at a time, or a finite group, and that the client sets the coaching agenda. What if we were to expand that view of who our clients are and the territory that coaching covers?

Coaching relationships and coaching skills have transformative power that could be employed to serve a broader agenda – that of building a world that works for everyone.

Although we often claim that coaches have no agenda of their own, this is rarely true. We typically hold many agendas for our clients – for example, we desire their self-care, fulfillment, life balance, career or business success, productivity, teamwork, and much more.

What would happen if we introduced into our coaching an agenda of global "self-care?" For example:

- When coaching people and organizations about their goals and plans, could we also hold the agenda of caring for the planet we all share?
- When coaching an organization's team, could we hold the agenda of not just their employer's success, but their impact on the community?
- When coaching in an industrialized country, could we also hold the agenda of the needs of the developing world?

Explore new perspectives about the world as your client with these resources:

"Coach the World" by Marquita Thompson

www.coachtheworld.blogspot.com/2008/12/coach-world.html

"Out of the Box, Into the World" by Virginia Kellogg

www.leadershipthatworks.com/utility/showArticle/?objectID=142

"Social Change through Coaching" by Janet Harvey

www.invitechange.com/blog/social-change-through-coaching/

"Why Lead?" by Henry Kimsey-House and David Skibbins

www.thecoaches.com/resources/multimedia/why-lead.html

"It's my belief that the world – the earth itself and all forms that exist upon it – is the coach's true client, not just the individuals you coach. I think coaching has emerged at this time in history in response to a call from the world. We need to redefine the concept of the 'client's agenda' to simultaneously hold the agenda of the world, the agenda of our clients, and our own agenda of creating a sustainable livelihood."

Virginia Kellogg, Troy, PA, brings coaching skills to nonprofits and communities. She was a co-creator of the Coaching and Philanthropy Project.

33. Choose a coach for yourself who shares your ideals.

● ●

Coaching can help anyone create change – even you.

If you are ready to start creating change in the world, one of the most powerful steps you can take in that direction is to work with a coach yourself. Coaching can help you build a personal vision of a better world, hold on to your changemaking agenda despite other demands and distractions, and break through barriers that block your effectiveness.

Choosing a coach who shares a vision or values similar to your own can add extra potency to the relationship. Look at it this way: if one of your key goals was to build your business, you might select a coach who emphasized financial success. Or if you were struggling with overwork, you might pick a coach who stressed life balance. Similarly, a coach who is actively engaged in changemaking could be the strong ally you need to bolster your own changemaking work.

Consider making this "changemaker quotient" part of what you evaluate when selecting your coach. A coach who has already taken a stand for change may be exactly the right one to take a stand for you.

Use referral sources like these to find a coach to hire:

Association for Coaching (U.K.)
www.associationforcoaching.com/dir/dir.htm

Coach U
www.findacoach.com

The Coaches Training Institute
www.coactivenetwork.com/webx?ctiFindACoach@@

International Association of Coaching
www.certifiedcoach.org/find.lasso

International Coach Federation
www.coachfederation.org/find-a-coach/

Or use these resources to find a peer coach at a low cost:

Coaches Coaching Circle
www.coachescoachingcircle.com

Reciprocoach
www.reciprocoach.com

"Find a coach who lives the life you imagine living and models what you would like to be doing. Choose someone who shares your values. Are you looking for someone who believes that the path to success is making a difference in the world? Or would you prefer to find someone who can just show you how to make a lot of money, no matter how you do it? I suspect you would rather work with someone who strives to empower others, since if you're reading this, that's probably YOUR goal, too."

Marjorie Geiser, Prescott, AZ, helps wellness professionals go from uncertainty to focus and clarity so they build their dream business.

34. Maximize your own coaching potential.

● ●

Make the most impact with your coaching by becoming the best coach you can be.

You may already be a good coach, but what if you could become great? And if you're masterful now, what might it take to stay that way?

Even if you have many years experience in a related field, a new coach can almost always benefit from some level of coach-specific training. For a coach who has been practicing for some time, continuing to develop your professional skills can increase your range and impact.

Plan for your professional development as a coach.

1. Determine where your "growing edge" is. What do you need most right now to be the best possible coach? Basic coaching skills? Help with some areas you find challenging? To refresh skills you learned in the past? Specialized techniques for your niche? Advanced training in new territory?

2. Decide what approach would work best for you to learn and develop what you need. Enroll in a comprehensive training program? Take a class or two? Hire a coach, supervisor, or mentor? Participate in a group? Learn from a book, audio, or video?

3. Find a provider through a trusted source. For example, directories published by groups you rely on, new programs offered by the school you attended, or classes, groups, coaches, and learning materials recommended by friends and colleagues.

These resources can help you choose a learning approach or training provider:

"Guidelines on Supervision" by European Mentoring & Coaching Council
www.emccouncil.org/src/ultimo/models/Download/7.pdf

International Association of Coaching: "Get Coach Training"
www.certifiedcoach.org/index.php/get_certified/learn/get_coach_traiing/

International Coach Federation Training Program Search Service
www.coachfederation.org/icfcredentials/program-search/

Peer Resources Directory of Coach Training Programs and Schools
www.peer.ca/coachingschools.html

"Once we're living our success and potential we've become the best version of ourselves. We're self-expressed. The experience is one of overwhelming release and satisfaction because we are sharing our gifts with the world. We are of service, and that feels good. We are each born with the mission to master our own life, to learn how to create it, live it, and leave it. Our ultimate life lesson is achieving mastery."

Zoran Todorovic, Copenhagen, Denmark, coaches people and organizations to achieve their profound potential. He is the founder of TNM Coaching.

35. Partner up for support and increased impact.

●●●●●●●●●●●●●●●●●●●●●●●●●●●●

Extend your reach and leverage your resources with partnerships and alliances.

You can make more of a difference in almost any area you choose by engaging others to partner with you in some way. With a partner, you have the potential to reach a wider audience, provide clients with a broader range of capabilities, and access resources you couldn't afford alone. You'll also gain the perspective, support, and accountability that working in partnership provides.

Partnerships, alliances, and joint ventures can take many different forms, for example:

- Two or more coaches can team up to offer coaching or group programs together.
- Coaches can partner with other professionals to provide complementary services as a package.
- A group of coaches can form a company or alliance to market and provide services under a single brand.
- A coach can partner with an organization or institution to offer coaching to their clients, employees, students, or members.
- A junior coach can work with a more senior coach to gain experience and exposure to a new audience.
- A group of coaches can band together to form a network or success team for mutual benefit.
- Coaches can develop referral partnerships with others who serve a similar target market.
- Coaches and others can market each other's services in return for a commission or affiliate fee.

Learn more about partnering from these resources:

"60 Ways to Collaborate with Others"
Audio Recording with Andrea J. Lee
http://ajlee.audioacrobat.com/download/60waystocollaborate.mp3

"Creative Collaborations" by Deborah Gallant
www.boldbusinessworks.com/wp-content/uploads/Choice-Collaboration-article.pdf

SmartMatch Alliances™ **by Judy F. Feld and Ernest F. Oriente**
www.coachingsuccess.com

"Wanted: 100 Referral Partners" by C.J. Hayden
www.getclientsnow.com/dec2004.htm

"As an independent coach, you might encounter challenges in filling your calendar or scaling up. As in any other profession, peer networks and references offer win-win solutions. Often, the best partnerships involve coaches with skills and talents that are complementary to each other. Other alliances could be between coaches from different regions or with specialists from related fields. I would encourage all coaches to 'seek help as often as you offer help!'"

Gopal "GD" Shrikanth is a leading CEO coach in India. He founded India's premier (1500+ members) business/executive coaching foundation and a 100+ member network of executive/leadership coaches.

36. Build a sustainable business or career of your own.

• •

If you want to remain of service to others, you need to put on your own oxygen mask first.

When you focus on helping others, it's easy to forget that you must also look after yourself. But if you're not earning a sustainable living, you won't be able to continue being of service.

If you're a self-employed coach and your business isn't supporting you, you may need more coaching clients, higher paying clients, or a different business model. Many coach entrepreneurs offer programs, products, and services other than just coaching, in order to increase or stabilize their income.

If you prefer to work as an employee, there are more internal coaching jobs available now than in the past. But you'll have to be diligent and creative to seek out appropriate job opportunities and get hired.

Employment and self-employment aren't mutually exclusive. You may be able to find a part-time or contract position while you're building your coaching business. Or work in coaching part-time while earning elsewhere.

Regardless of how you go about it, you must have a realistic plan to support yourself financially. If you take care of the money first, it will be there to take care of you.

The following resources will help you build a successful coaching business or find a coaching job:

The Business of Coaching by Dorcas Kelley
www.thebusinessofcoaching.com

The Business and Practice of Coaching
by Lynn Grodzki and Wendy Allen
www.privatepracticesuccess.com

Get Clients Now! A 28-Day Marketing Program for Professionals, Consultants, and Coaches **by C.J. Hayden**
www.getclientsnow.com

International Coach Federation Career Centre
www.coachfederation.org/icf-members/assets-and-tools/icf-career-centre/

Marketing Essentials for Coaches **by Steve Mitten**
www.acoach4u.com

Multiple Streams of Coaching Income
by Andrea J. Lee
www.wealthythoughtleader.com/store/

"If you're like most coaches, you were drawn to this profession because you like helping people. But the truth is you can't help many people if you can't support yourself. Way too many good coaches struggle financially. If self-employment isn't the path for you, save yourself some suffering and explore other possibilities. A partnership? Internal coaching? And if you want to be successful as a self-employed coach, commit to do what it takes to build a profitable practice."

Steve Mitten, Vancouver, Canada, is a business and leadership coach. He was the 2005 president of the International Coach Federation.

PART III:
CHANGE THE WORLD BY BRINGING CHANGE TO OTHERS

• •

Creating change as a coach starts with you and your coaching business or career. But it doesn't have to end there. You can bring change to a wider audience by reaching out to new people and places, enrolling others in your changemaking vision, and transforming those you touch into changemakers in their own right.

There's a lot you can do on your own, but you can accomplish much more when you make the effort to also influence others. You can share your vision of change by educating, inspiring, advocating, providing tools and resources, or demonstrating what's possible.

Ideas can be contagious. Each person you influence has the ability to spread new ways of thinking and doing to everyone they reach. When you make use of the power of people to multiply your efforts, one person really can change the world.

37. Transform managers, executives, and leaders into coaches.

● ●

Change the culture of organizations by helping their leaders to become coaches.

You already know how powerful coaching can be as a tool for transformation. Imagine a world where every organization is led by people trained and experienced in using coaching skills.

Leaders who coach have the ability and mindset to inspire, motivate, champion, and challenge those on their team to develop their full potential. Our complex, rapidly-changing world needs people who work best independently, creatively, and flexibly, and that is exactly the work environment that a coaching culture can provide.

When leaders model a coaching approach, their teams learn and experience collaboration, mutual trust, adaptability, and resiliency. What better conditions could one have for fostering change?

Here are some of the ways you can help organizations to adopt a coaching culture:

- Train leaders in coaching skills to use on the job.
- Coach leaders in applying coaching skills in the workplace to become coaching role models.
- Offer team coaching to organizations to provide a shared experience of coaching for all participants.
- Train and coach people at all levels to become peer coaches for each other.
- Write, speak, and teach about coaching as a management and leadership tool.

Learn more about turning leaders into coaches from these resources:

Coaching for Leadership **by Marshall Goldsmith and Laurence S. Lyons, editors**
www.marshallgoldsmithlibrary.com

"Creating Coaching Cultures" by Merrill Anderson, Candice Frankovelgia, and Gina Hernez-Broome
www.ccl.org/leadership/pdf/research/CoachingCultures.pdf

The Heart of Coaching **by Thomas G. Crane**
www.craneconsulting.com

"Leaders Who Coach" by Teri Aulph
www.leadchangegroup.com/leaders-who-coach/

"Throughout my 20-year voyage within the corporate environment, I discovered the key to becoming an extraordinary leader was to be a great coach. The only leaders that ever had a significant impact on me and my career were those that adopted a coach approach. My own transformation from manager to leader-as-coach gave me the incentive to reach out and teach this powerful leadership quality to those ready for extraordinary success."

Frank Traditi, Highlands Ranch, CO, is an executive leadership development coach. He has been a senior leader and coached executives and managers in five Fortune 500 corporations.

38. Bring coaching to people and places where it's unknown.

● ●

Discover new frontiers for coaches and coaching to explore.

How might it change the world if there were coaches on staff at the White House? Or for Parliament? If every United Nations ambassador was assigned a coach? If there was a coach for every schoolteacher? If our prisons employed coaches? Or our armed forces?

What if every corporate social responsibility department included a coach? Or every police department? What if coaching skills were taught in kindergarten? Or in our legal system? Or to every participant in peace talks worldwide?

Where could you take coaching that it's never been before? What populations need coaching but have no access to it? What institutions could be changed for the better by employing coaches? Where might coaching cause widespread transformation it if were adopted?

Consider how you could broaden the horizons for coaching by taking it into unknown territory. Millions could benefit because you imagined a new frontier for coaching and took action on your ideas.

Explore these examples of new territory for coaching:

"The Coach Initiative: Volunteer Coaches Making A Difference" by Diane Krause-Stetson
www.certifiedcoachblog.typepad.com/blog/2009/03/the-coach-initiativevolunteer-coaches-making-a-difference.html

"Coaching & Workplace Violence" by Mark Joyella
www.coachingcommons.org/featured/coaching-and-workplace-violence-a-critical-tool-in-prevention-and-recovery/

Results Coaching: The New Essential for School Leaders **by Kathryn Kee, Karen Anderson, et al.**
www.coachingforresultsglobal.com/resources.html

Foundation for International Leadership Coaching
www.leadershipcoachingfoundation.org

Laura Whitworth Prison Project
www.prisonproject.org

"NGO Use of Coaching Interventions" by Lynne Gilliland and Robert A. Jud
www.gillilandjud.com/pdfs/NGO_Coaching_Booklet.pdf

"I saw that coaching was an enormous opportunity for Russia, because our country was in a situation where in a short time we had to find the most effective ways to integrate into the global economy. We did not have many resources that we could use for this, and with so many needs, things were very tight. With coaching, we could develop the potential of our greatest resource – our people."

Svetlana Chumakova, Moscow, is the only Master Certified Coach in Russia. Her International Coaching Academy brought coaching to Russia in 1998.

39. Provide other coaches with the tools they need to make a difference.

• •

Magnify the impact of coaching by empowering other coaches to create change.

If you believe that coaching can make a difference in the world, imagine how you might expand its reach if every coach had access to the tools they needed to coach changemakers, bring coaching to new environments, and start making change themselves.

Consider these possibilities for providing the tools of change to other coaches:

- Publish a book, white paper, case study, or article on coaching for social change or coaching underserved populations.
- Develop a training program to teach group, team, or peer coaching for new audiences, or teach coaching skills to non-coach leaders.
- Offer a system or service for matching volunteer coaches with pro bono or low-cost recipients.
- Design a toolkit to help coaches expand their changemaking work. For example: tools to use with clients, for conducting trainings, or with the media.

Here are some examples of tools created to help coaches make a difference:

"Lessons from Rwanda" by Victoria Trabosh

www.victoriatrabosh.com/wp-content/uploads/2012/01/Trabosh-CHOICE-article-April-2008.pdf

Coaching and Philanthropy Project Toolkit
https://groups.compasspoint.org/coachingnonprofits/

"Delivering a 'Coaching Toolbox' to the Remote Villages of the World" by Mark Joyella
www.coachingtheglobalvillage.org/in-the-news/hello-world/

The Fork: Connecting the Deeper Inside with the Larger Outside by Rudy Vandamme
www.ecologize.net

One to One: Women Coaching Women
www.onetoone.info

"Serving Pro Bono Clients While Building a Profitable Coaching Business" by Meg Montford
www.abilitiesenhanced.com/pro-bono.html

"This is an important issue and one we take very seriously at *choice, the magazine of professional coaching*. Considering that coaching is in its infancy as a profession, it is a mandate to all of us in this amazing industry to provide tools and support to those who are making this a viable business. We continue to look for content from writers and guest speakers to provide learning and application that serves as a stepping stone to success."

Garry Schleifer is a business development coach based in Toronto, Canada. He is the publisher of choice, the magazine of professional coaching *which provides tools to coaches worldwide.*

40. Advocate for positive change in the organizations where you work.

• •

Influence the organizations that employ you to make changes for the better.

Whether you serve an organization as an employee or a service provider, your influence can make a difference. Do you think your employer or client should show more responsibility to the environment? Provide better benefits for their employees? Ensure that their suppliers provide humane working conditions? Give more back to their community? Speak up about what you see and suggest possibilities for change.

As an employee, you might:

- Serve on an employee council for green practices, social responsibility, or employee affairs, or start one if none exist.
- Launch a community volunteer service program for employees of your organization.
- Ask for reusable or recyclable cups and utensils, and organic and local food, in break rooms and cafeterias.
- Advocate for telecommuting wherever it's feasible.

As a service provider, you might:

- Suggest that social benefit topics be included in the organization's strategic planning sessions.
- Educate clients about the bottom-line benefits of becoming more socially responsible.
- Propose a cause marketing approach for a product launch or promotional campaign.
- Refuse to participate in projects you perceive as being harmful or unethical.

These resources can help you create change in the organizations where you work:

Evolved Employer Blog by Nicki Gilmour and Melissa Anderson

www.evolvedemployer.com

Green Your Work by Kim Carlson

www.earthsmartconsumer.com

Saving the World at Work by Tim Sanders

www.timsanders.com

Cause marketing resources, page 21

Sources for socially-responsible vendors, pages 18-19

"The challenge is to help leaders and their organizations increase corporate responsibility: achieving business objectives in ways that contribute to the sustainability and development of the countries, workforces, and communities they impact. Our influence is most powerful when we too are responsible – seeing the whole picture, respecting multinationals' needs equally with stakeholders we want served. When aligned respectfully – even humbly – with what is, we can help clients make ongoing improvement toward what can be."

Beth Hand is a consultant and executive coach in Alexandria, VA. She helps corporations doing business in emerging markets increase their corporate responsibility.

41. Ask your membership organizations to increase their social responsibility.

● ●

Use your influence as a member to promote positive change in the groups you belong to.

As a member of a professional or trade association, alumni network, or networking group, you have an opportunity to prompt widespread change. When an organization announces new, more socially responsible practices to their membership, it has a ripple effect, convincing other members to make similar changes, and to bring them to still more businesses and organizations.

Consider asking your membership organizations to make changes like these:

- Adopt green practices for meetings and conferences, such as providing downloadable handouts, eliminating bottled water and beverages, avoiding disposable plates and utensils, and offering recycling.
- Schedule events in locations easily accessible by mass transit, or provide for carpooling.
- Host speakers on social responsibility, sustainability, or making a difference in the community.
- Establish community service projects or charitable giving programs for members to participate in.
- Set up a pro bono service bureau for members to donate their professional time to people and organizations in need.
- Showcase the efforts of members and their businesses to give back and practice social responsibility.
- Publicly advocate for change on issues relevant to the group's members and their concerns.

Explore these resources for helping membership organizations promote social responsibility and change:

ASAE Global Principles for Socially Responsible Associations

www.asaecenter.org/Forms/SocialResponsibilityPrincipl es/index.cfm

MeetingsNet Give Back Portal

www.meetingsnet.com/give-back/

National & Community Service Resource Ctr

www.nationalserviceresources.org

U.N. Global Compact Green Meeting Guide

www.unglobalcompact.org/docs/issues_doc/Environme nt/Green_Meeting_Guide_WEB.pdf

"Living and working from values is often the reason so many of us became coaches and our clients come to us. They are also key to fostering sustainability and social responsibility at work and in organizations. Ask yourself if, as an organization, you are living the values and intentions you profess? If not, what needs to change? What would honoring those values look like? How can you use the strength of numbers to influence change?"

Matthew Rochte, Chicago, IL, is director of corporate sustainability and responsibility at Opportunity Sustainability. He has been coaching executives on business sustainability since 1991.

42. Use your blog or social networks to advocate for good.

● ●

A few words and a link can transform a ripple into a sea change.

You no longer need to be a journalist to have an audience of readers listening to what you say. If you author a blog, post to social networks like Facebook, LinkedIn, Twitter, or Google+, belong to online discussion groups or message boards, or create content for YouTube or SlideShare, you have the potential to deliver your message of change to hundreds or even thousands.

There are dozens of ways you can advocate for good online:

- Inform your blog readers and social networks about important issues and stimulate discussion.
- Tell stories about people who are affected by an issue or working to do something about it.
- Publish interviews with people representing a cause or invite them to guest blog for you.
- Invite your contacts to meetups, rallies, fundraisers, lectures, or screenings.
- Ask contacts to take action by joining a network, writing letters, making calls, voting on an issue, or telling friends about it.
- Raise funds for a charity or cause.
- Use photos, videos, slides, or graphic images to communicate complex ideas more impactfully.
- Make use of humor and you'll encourage others to share your posts. Publish issue-oriented cartoons, jokes, satire, or parodies.

These resources will help you become more effective at online advocacy:

10 Tactics for Turning Information into Action
Video by Tactical Technology Collective
www.informationactivism.org

Meta-Activism Project
www.meta-activism.org

The Networked Nonprofit **by Beth Kanter and Allison Fine**
www.bethkanter.org

Quick 'n' Easy Guide to Online Advocacy
www.onlineadvocacy.tacticaltech.org

"So many of us go through our lives remaining silent about what really matters to us, the world, and other people. It is as if we are on auto-pilot, day after day. It is so easy to become indifferent, remain silent, and not do anything about some of the huge challenges the world faces today – such as social injustice, poverty, famine, global warming, diminishing resources, and so on. It's now time to stop being silent. Look around your life today and see where you are being silent – and ask yourself why."

Arvind Devalia is a London, England coach. In his blog "Make It Happen: for a Better You & a Better World" he writes on living an inspired life, personal social responsibility and changing the world.

43. Make your social change activities public.

• •

Share what you're doing and you'll inspire others to follow your example.

D on't be embarrassed to toot your own horn if you are actively contributing to building a better world. Your colleagues and community will be inspired when they hear about your changemaking activities. Are you volunteering, offering pro bono coaching, donating a portion of your income, greening your business? Let people know and they just may follow your example.

Here are some ways you can encourage others to act by sharing what action you're taking:

- When you volunteer, donate, or take action on behalf of a cause, blog about it, tweet it, or post it to your social network status to let others know.

- Add a "social responsibility" page to your website, summarizing everything you do to give back to your community or protect the environment.

- Send a news release to your local media, trade press, or professional association about your social change activities.

- If one of the ways you express social responsibility is to work with clients engaged in social change, let people know that you coach activists, or nonprofits, or social enterprises, and why.

- Use speaking engagements or interviews to talk about changemaking. Of course describe your work as a coach, but mention your social change work also.

Consider these examples of coaches making their social responsibility activities public:

Action COACH's Coaching for a Cause

www.coachingforacause.org

Belma González's website

www.bcoachingandconsulting.com/about.php

Denver Business Journal: "For Business Coach Korbel, Social Responsibility Is a Given"

www.bizjournals.com/denver/stories/2006/08/21/focus4.html

Focal Point Coaching website

www.focalpointcoaching.com/news-media/responsibility

IMA Journal: "How C.J. Hayden Structured Her Business to Focus on Social Change"

www.cjhayden.com/content/CJ-Hayden-IMA-Journal.pdf

Life Coaching for Battered Women: Interviews with Deborah Nesbit

http://youtu.be/36H5N9eUrNY **and** www.coachfederation.org/includes/media/docs/aprilcare.pdf

The Performance Coach website

www.theperformancecoach.com/csr/

Zane Green's website

www.happivate.com/about_us.php?#Environmental

44. Write, speak, and teach about your ideals.

● ●

Use your skills as an educator to inform and inspire other changemakers.

Coaches are frequently natural educators. Many of us write articles and books, speak at meetings and conferences, and teach workshops and classes. Why not make use of these influential skills to help make the world a better place?

You can perform a valuable service to your community and the world by raising people's awareness about important issues, advocating for a cause, or informing others what action they can take.

Consider these possibilities for educating others about causes, issues, and social change topics:

- Write articles for newsletters, blogs, magazines, webzines, or professional journals.
- Write letters to the editor or guest editorials.
- Write a white paper, case study, or action guide.
- Write a book, or contribute a chapter to one.
- Give talks at local community groups, professional associations, libraries, or schools.
- Offer brown-bag lunch talks to companies and organizations.
- Speak for teleseminars, webinars, or online chats.
- Lead a breakout session at a conference, serve on a panel, or deliver a keynote.
- Organize a community workshop or teach-in.
- Teach a class through a university extended education department or community resource center.

These resources can help you educate others about social change topics:

The Activist Toolkit Wiki: Public Speaking
www.activist-toolkit.wikispaces.com/Public+Speaking

Leading Out Loud **by Terry Pearce**
www.terrypearce.com

Writing to Change the World **by Mary Pipher**
www.marypipher.net

Writing to Make a Difference **by Dalya F. Massachi**
www.dfmassachi.net

"You have a passion, a unique message, something that you can share like no one else. The time has come for you to not only share it, but to attract to yourself a community of followers that are also passionate about this cause or problem or dream – and want to join you in its fulfillment. The gifts you offer are exactly what a particular group of people – perfectly matched to your message – needs to hear, see and experience now. Being a thought leader is not just for CEOs and 'top dogs' – it's for anyone who wants to be a force of influence, inspiration, and impact."

Marcia Bench, Scottsdale, AZ, founded the Career Coach Institute. She is a teacher, speaker, and author of 24 books, including **Become an Inspirational Thought Leader.**

45. Join a group of changemakers.

● ●

Boost your world-changing ability by joining with others on a similar path.

Changing the world doesn't have to be a lonely occupation. In fact, you are much more likely to sustain your efforts if you stay connected with other changemakers.

Being part of a group can provide you with moral support, inspiration, new information, added resources, accountability, and camaraderie.

Here are some avenues for finding like-minded others to confer, conspire, or collaborate with:

- Join an association, community group, or online network dedicated to changemaking overall or to specific issues you care about.
- Seek out like-minded changemakers via membership directories, message boards, and social networks.
- Look for changemaking groups and events in local activity calendars.
- Volunteer for a cause that interests you and you'll meet others who share your views.
- Start a group or event of your own in your local area or on your favorite online network.
- Enter a competition for changemaking ideas; you'll meet the organizers, judges, and other participants.

Find other changemakers through resources like these:

Business Alliance for Local Living Economies
www.livingeconomies.org

Care2
www.care2.com

Citizens for Global Solutions
www.globalsolutions.org

The Hub
www.the-hub.net

Idealist
www.idealist.org

Justmeans
www.justmeans.com

Meetup
www.meetup.com

Net Impact
www.netimpact.org

"Joining groups of changemakers has been the single most beneficial tactic I've used to build my coaching practice. 90% of my clients have come from meetings of like-minded people. The business opportunities are greatest when I'm a presenter, but I meet clients simply by attending. These groups have also helped me flourish through the camaraderie, support, and inspiration I receive from these relationships, many of which become life-long friendships."

Sara Ellis Conant is a San Francisco, CA leadership coach. She is a lifetime member of Net Impact and founder of Young Women Social Entrepreneurs.

46. Blow the whistle on unethical or irresponsible practices.

● ●

Speak out against corruption, fraud, abuse, and dangers to health, safety, and our planet.

One of the most powerful tools for change you have is your own voice. When you protest misconduct, you shine a light on it, revealing it to the world. Your whistle-blowing raises public awareness and encourages others to follow your example. When enough people speak out, change happens, in the form of public pressure to reform, violators being prosecuted, and new legislation.

Consider these ideas for blowing the whistle:

- Report the offender to the appropriate government agency or enforcement authority.
- Contact your political representatives, asking them to support legislation or demand prosecution.
- Spread the word to friends and colleagues through emails, phone calls, and social media.
- Alert the media, including newspapers, magazines, radio, television, reporters, columnists, and bloggers.
- Contact the leaders of offending companies or organizations and call for change.
- Join a group established to fight the type of abuse that concerns you.
- Report ethical violations to the appropriate governing body for the perpetrator's industry or field.
- Consult an attorney about bringing an individual or class action lawsuit.
- Support your coaching clients in taking any of the above actions to right the wrongs they see.

Explore these resources to help with whistleblowing:

Giving Voice to Values **by Mary C. Gentile**
www.givingvoicetovaluesthebook.com

Int'l Coach Federation Ethical Conduct Review
www.coachfederation.org/about-icf/ethics/independent-review-process/

LawGuru: Free Legal Advice Online
www.lawguru.com

Moral Courage in Organizations: Doing the Right Thing at Work **by Debra R. Comer and Gina Vega**
www.sharpe-etext.com/product/moral-courage-in-organizations19854

National Whistleblowers Center (U.S.)
www.whistleblowers.org

"It takes courage to be a whistleblower. You aren't often thanked for it, but if you aspire to 'higher order' values, you will do it. What distinguishes the ordinary from the extraordinary is seeing what is wrong and doing something about it. Sometimes the best action is to offer a quiet word to the offenders; in other circumstances you may need to alert the appropriate authority. The world won't change to the better unless you try to right the wrongs you see."

Dr. Stephen Treloar is a Sydney, Australia executive coach and mentor. With a background in commercial law, mediation, and university lecturing, he speaks frequently on leadership and business ethics.

47. Participate in crowdsourcing strategies for change.

● ●

Collaborate online with other motivated changemakers.

Crowdsourcing allows large numbers of people in far-flung locations to collaborate on generating ideas, analyzing problems, and designing solutions. With Internet-based collaboration, group intelligence can be applied to seemingly intractable issues.

In crowdsourcing, an idea or problem is broadcast to a community, and its members devise solutions to the issue or approaches to implementing the idea. The "crowd" votes to select the best submissions, or the crowdsourcer chooses the ones they like best. Then the crowdsourcer or another member of the community puts the ideas and solutions to work.

You can get involved in crowdsourcing by submitting ideas regarding issues that concern you, voting on ideas others have submitted, or performing a task an organization needs done in order to further its goals.

Some examples: The U.S. Federal Communications Commission is currently collecting ideas from the public on how to best improve the country's broadband infrastructure at www.broadband.ideascale.com.

In 2009, the U.K. newspaper *The Guardian* enlisted the help of 20,000 citizens to search expense claim documents from Members of Parliament to find out-of-line claims.

SeeClickFix.com collects reports from citizens on neighborhood issues and makes them available to the media and government officials in 25,000 towns.

Learn more about participating in crowdsourcing from these resources:

Ashoka Changemakers
www.changemakers.com

Building Blocks for Building Communities
http://ourblocks.net

Crowdsourcing.org
www.crowdsourcing.org

Innovation Exchange
www.innovationexchange.com

Ushahidi's Crowdmap
www.crowdmap.com

Worldchanging.com
www.worldchanging.com

"We use crowdsourcing to design our coaching programs to be a perfect fit for our clients. For example, we used crowdsourcing to design our last training program, which helped heart-centered business owners in 22 countries learn how to create teleseminars to spread their message to more people. The collective wisdom of 300 clients helped us determine each module of our program better than we could have done ourselves."

Patrick Dominguez is a marketing coach in San Francisco, CA, who regularly designs coaching programs using crowdsourcing.

48. Start a social change project of your own.

● ●

Assemble your own team of worldchangers and put them to work.

L aunching your own social change project can be highly rewarding, personally empowering, and create a substantial impact. It can also require a great deal of time and money, duplicate the efforts of others, and not produce the results you hoped for.

The best way to approach launching a new project is to first consider carefully your personal situation and desires, the impact you want to have, and the resources you can access. Social change projects can be as simple as you and a few friends getting together to do some good, or as complex as starting a new company or organization.

Consider how you might assemble a team of friends, family, colleagues, and/or clients to:

- Volunteer as a group to help a worthy cause.
- Donate a block of money, time, or professional services to an organization you support.
- Pitch in to solve a problem in your community.
- Pledge to take specific action about an issue and recruit others to do the same.
- Contact the media, political representatives, or leaders of offending companies to call for change.
- Produce a blog, book, video, or film to call attention to a problem or solution.
- Demonstrate for or against an important issue.
- Form an association, company, or nonprofit to achieve change in a new and different way.

These resources can help you launch your own project:

Change.org

www.change.org

The Creative Activist Toolkit

www.creativevisions.org/2011/07/creative-activist-toolkit/

"How to Spark and Build a Social Movement" by Susannah Vila

www.movements.org/how-to/entry/buildamovement

National Service Resource Center

www.nationalserviceresources.org

Resources for taking action, page 26

"There is no shortage of possible projects you could undertake to uplift your community while uplifting yourself and your business at the same time. Ask yourself if there is a cause or group you would like to be more involved with that could use some help. When you give back to the community, you also feed your soul, participate in a great opportunity for personal growth, and have a lot of fun. Start today to involve yourself in your community and both will benefit."

Caterina Rando is a business coach, speaker, and publisher based in San Francisco, CA. She founded the nonprofit A Good Deed Tea.

49. Commit to playing a bigger game.

● ●

Challenge your limitations and become willing to step into your own greatness.

In the words of Marianne Williamson, "Your playing small does not serve the world."If you truly want to make the world a better place, you may need to take on bigger challenges than you have before. What if you are the one whose ideas and efforts could change everything, and you choose not to act because you are too busy, or afraid, or think you're not good enough?

Mohandas Gandhi was a mediocre lawyer from a middle-class family who barely passed his college exams. Nelson Mandela ran away from home, was thrown out of college, and was fired from his first job. Mother Teresa was a middle-aged high school teacher with no funding of any kind when she began helping the poor.

Albert Schweitzer was a church deacon and organist who used his concert fees to earn a medical degree at the age of 36 and found a hospital in Africa. Pioneering social reformer Jane Addams never finished college and suffered from poor health her entire life. Trade union leader Lech Walesa was an unemployed shipyard worker with no higher education, whose activism on behalf of workers won him the Nobel Peace Prize and the presidency of Poland.

You know the names of these heroes because they decided to play a bigger game. Despite all the reasons they might have thought there was nothing they could do, no one would listen, or their dreams were too impossible, they took action. And as a result, millions of lives were changed for the better.

Explore these resources to help you play a bigger game:

A Return to Love **by Marianne Williamson**
www.mariannewilliamson.com

The Bigger Game® **by Laura Whitworth, Rick Tamlyn, and Caroline MacNeill Hall**
www.thebiggergame.com

The Impossible Will Take a Little While **by Paul Rogat Loeb**
www.paulloeb.org

Blessed Unrest: **Video with Paul Hawken**
http://youtu.be/npKaOddyrcY

TED Talks
http://www.ted.com

"Bigger Games are what change the world from what it is now to what it could be. Yes, that's a lofty claim. And yet, it is proven true all the time, as people no different from you and me leave indelible handprints on their companies, their communities, their neighborhoods, their countries, and their planet... Playing a Bigger Game is about being absorbed in something worthy and hot that pulls on your soul and lights up your life."

Rick Tamlyn, Hague, NY, is an executive coach, keynote speaker, and coach trainer. He is co-author of **The Bigger Game,** *and leads Bigger Game workshops internationally.*

50. Spread the word.

● ●

Share the ideas in this book with others.

Throughout this book, you've been reading about concrete ways that coaches can change the world. Perhaps you've chosen one approach, or several, to take action about. Here's one simple thing you can do right now to make a difference – tell other coaches about this book and the ideas it contains.

At a coaching conference one day, a representative for a personality assessment firm revealed the following. After giving their test for many years at professional conferences around the world, they discovered that the coaching profession had the highest concentration of altruists they had ever seen in one place.

That's who we coaches are – people unselfishly concerned for the welfare of others. Imagine what a difference we can make by devoting an entire profession's energy to solving the world's problems.

Here are some ways you can help spread the word:

- Tell your coaching friends and colleagues about this book and what it has motivated you to do.
- Post about this book on Facebook, Twitter, LinkedIn, Google+, and any other social network or message board you belong to.
- Blog about some of the book's ideas or include them in a podcast.
- Mention the book in an article or interview for a coaching publication or website.
- Review the book on Amazon.com, Goodreads.com, Smashwords.com, or any coaching resource website.
- Give copies of this book as gifts to other coaches.

- Put this book on the resource list of your website or class handout.
- Visit the book's website and add to our resource lists or tell your own story of changemaking.

Remember that for every copy of this book sold, another dollar is donated to the International Coach Federation Foundation, making coaching and coach training available to those who can't afford it.

Coaches *can* change the world. And change begins with you.

Visit our website:

50 Ways Coaches Can Change the World
www.coacheschangetheworld.com

"Through spreading the skills that coaches use, asking not telling, pulling not pushing, into normal management behaviour in larger institutions like education, healthcare, the military and the prison service, personal responsibility will grow and with it the freedom to choose. This is indeed the evolutionary journey that will eventually leave the power hungry starving, and the world a better place."

Sir John Whitmore, London, England, is often called the godfather of coaching. His book **Coaching for Performance** *has sold 500,000 copies in 17 languages. He co-founded the Be the Change Symposium.*

HOW TO GET STARTED

••••••••••••••••••••••••••

Ihope you have enjoyed reading the ideas shared in this book. Even more, I hope they have inspired you to consider taking some action of your own. You may already be traveling along a world-changing path, but perhaps you are now thinking of tackling something new, or expanding your efforts. Here are some suggestions to help you get started.

Choosing Your Path

There are so many people and places in our world that need help. Deciding where to direct your world-changing energies can be quite a challenge. There are typically four factors you'll want to consider:

1. **What** issues you will focus on. You might define this by the needs you see, problems you want solved, or goals you think should be achieved.
2. **Who** you wish to support. This may be a group of people defined by need, location, or demographics. It could also be a group of animals or an element of the natural environment.
3. **How** to best make a contribution. This will depend on your natural talents, core competencies, personal interests, or professional skills and training. It could also depend on the assets you have available – a large mailing list, for example, or space to hold events.
4. **Where** to begin. It may take some time to achieve your ultimate goals. You'll need a likely place to start.

To bring more clarity to those four aspects of your mission, ask yourself the following questions:

- What problems or goals inspire you the most?
- What kinds of stories or issues give you the urge to do something?
- What gifts or resources do you have to share?
- How much time or money can you contribute?
- Would you rather work alone or with others?
- What past experience or existing connections could help you?

Draft a preliminary mission statement for your world-changing project that includes the four what, who, how, and where factors. Share it with some like-minded friends or colleagues and see what they think. Refine your mission based on their feedback and your reaction to what they say.

Beginning Your Journey

If your project is simple and straightforward, you can start acting immediately. You won't need much planning or support to implement new practices like buying recycled paper or volunteering at your local food bank.

But many world-changing projects require more investigation or preparation. If you are considering a significant new effort, such as changing your coaching niche or starting a charitable initiative at your company, here are some ways you might approach it:

1. Research the field and the players. Who is serving this need, group, or cause already? How? Where? Learn more about the area you want to work in and see who is already involved and what they are doing.
2. Design your unique contribution. How can you do something different than others are already doing? Or

how can you add to their efforts collaboratively? Try out your idea on some people already engaged in the field, and revise it based on their suggestions.

3. Reach out to potential team members. If you've decided you want to work with others, present some possible candidates with your mission statement and project idea and see if they would like to participate. Ask what they might contribute.

5. Develop your project's model. Try on different ways of accomplishing your mission that could make good use of your unique contribution. Ask your team to help you. Examine others in the field and compare your goals and situation to theirs. Keep looking and talking and revising until you have what you believe is a good fit.

6. Identify possible funding sources. Many projects require funding of some kind. Once you have a model in mind, start to identify possible funding sources. How much will you need to get your project off the ground? Where can you obtain that kind of funding? What will be required to get it?

7. Prepare an action plan. Now you should be ready to create a plan of action. What will you do? By when? What help do you need? When do you want to launch and how long will it take you to be ready?

Staying the Course

World-changing can be exhilarating and rewarding. It can also be tiring and stressful. Seek out ongoing sources of logistical, emotional, and spiritual support, and make liberal use of them. When you take good care of yourself, you'll be better able to care for others.

The following resources can help with your world-changing efforts:

The Activist Toolkit Wiki
www.activist-toolkit.wikispaces.com

Change.org
www.change.org

Citizen You **by Jonathan Tisch and Karl Weber**
www.citizenyou.org

Coaching and Philanthropy Project Toolkit
https://groups.compasspoint.org/coachingnonprofits/

Coaching for Transformation: Pathways to Ignite Personal and Social Change **by Martha Lasley, Virginia Kellogg, Richard Michaels, and Sharon Brown**
www.leadershipthatworks.com/Public/Products/

Giving **by Bill Clinton**
http://giving.clintonfoundation.org

The Lifelong Activist **by Hillary Rettig**
www.hillaryrettig.com/books/

Starting & Building a Nonprofit **by Peri Pakroo**
www.peripakroo.com/books/

Venture Forth **by Rolfe Larson**
www.rolfelarson.com

VolunteerMatch
www.volunteermatch.org

DISCUSSION QUESTIONS

• •

If you have found the ideas in this book valuable, consider discussing them with other coaches. You might form a book study group to read the book and discuss it together. Or dedicate a meeting of your coaching chapter, community of practice, or special interest group to discussing these ideas. Below are some questions you can use as the basis of your discussion.

1. What does "changing the world" mean to you, and why is this important?
2. How did reading about the 50 ways make you feel? What thoughts were inspired in you?
3. If you were to add a 51st way for coaches to change the world, what would it be?
4. Which of the 50 ways might you disagree with, and how would you improve them?
5. Which of the 50 ways are you already engaged in?
6. If you were to take on a new one of the 50 ways to engage in, which one would you choose?
7. Which of the 50 ways address what you believe are the most pressing issues in your community or the world?
8. Which of the 50 ways would make the best use of the unique gifts you possess?
9. Which of the 50 ways might help you build your business or boost your career?
10. What examples can you think of that illustrate coaches who are using any of these approaches?

11. What resources do world-changing coaches most need, and where might they find them?
12. How can a coach engaged in world-changing stay motivated and inspired?
13. How might your group of coaches engage in world-changing together?
14. What strengths or resources does your group possess that could benefit your community or the world?
15. How might your group of coaches make the most positive impact on the community within which you coach?
16. What other world-changing groups might your group partner with to increase its impact?
17. What action would you like to commit to as a result of this discussion?

CONTRIBUTORS

● ●

My grateful thanks to all the coaches who made this book possible, including those whose names I haven't mentioned. Below are all those whose perspectives were quoted on each of the 50 ways.

Marcia Bench, JD, CCMP
Author, Speaker & Coach
www.marciabench.com

Neela Bettridge
Leadership Coach & Sustainability Advisor
www.neelabettridge.com

Mrim Boutla, Ph.D.
Co-Founder, More Than Money Careers
www.morethanmoneycareers.com

Rhonda Britten
Founder, Fearless Living Institute
www.fearlessliving.com

Vikki Brock, Ph.D., EMBA, MCC
Leadership Coach & Author
www.vikkibrock.com

Charles Brook
Founder & Managing Director, The Performance Coach
www.theperformancecoach.com

Kay Cannon, MBA, MCC
Executive Coach
www.kaycannon.com

Breeze Carlile, CPCC
President, It's A Breeze Moving Gracefully
www.itsabreezemoving.com

Svetlana Chumakova, MCC
Co-Founder, International Coaching Academy
www.coacha.ru

Ginger Cockerham, CMC, MCC
Principal, Cockerham Coaching Group, LLC
www.coachginger.com

Sara Ellis Conant, MBA
Leadership Coach
www.saraellisconant.com

Veronica Conway, CPCC
Coach & Facilitator
 www.veronicaconway.com

Arvind Devalia, MBA
Coach, Author, Speaker, & Social Media Consultant
www.arvinddevalia.com

Patrick Dominguez, MS
Marketing Coach
www.billbaren.com

Ryan Eliason
CEO, Professional Coaching Inc.
www.ryaneliason.com

Dave Ellis
Founder, Brande Foundation
www.thecoachingproject.org

Hide Enomoto, CPCC
Founder, Seven Generations
www.changethedream.jp

Monica J. Foster, CC, CVBC, CPSS, RM
The Life Beyond Limits® Coach
www.butterflywheel.com

Joan Friedlander
Principal, Lifework Business Partners
www.joanfriedlander.com

Dolly M. Garlo, RN, JD, Board Certified Coach
Business Development & Career Transition
www.creatinglegacy.com

Marjorie Geiser, MBA, RD
Business Coach for Health & Fitness Professionals
www.meg-enterprises.com

Beth Hand, MBA
Consultant & Executive Coach
www.leadershiphand.com

Ruth Ann Harnisch
President, the Harnisch Foundation
www.thehf.org

Gina Hayden, MSc, PCC, CCI
Director, The Conscious Leadership Consultancy
www.theconsciousleadershipconsultancy.com

Reuel J. Hunt
Founder, Coaching Kids
www.coachingkids.org

Carlo J. Jensen, BComm, CEC, PCC
Executive Coach
www.uniscan.ca

Shana Montesol Johnson, MPP, ACC
Career & Executive Coach
www.developmentcrossroads.com

Donna Karlin, CEC, Diplomate IABMCP
Founder, A Better Perspective®
www.abetterperspective.com

Virginia Kellogg, MCC, CPCC
Leadership Coach
www.leadershipthatworks.com

Karen Kimsey-House, MCC, CPCC
Co-Founder, The Coaches Training Institute
www.thecoaches.com

Steve Mitten, CPCC, MCC
Business & Leadership Coach
www.acoach4u.com

David Matthew Prior, MBA, MCC, BCC
President of Getacoach.com
www.getacoach.com

Caterina Rando, MA, MCC, CPCC
Business Coach, Speaker & Publisher
www.attractclientswithease.com

Ann Ranson
Executive Coach & Marketing Consultant
www.annranson.com

Hillary Rettig
Coach & Activist
www.hillaryrettig.com

Matthew Rochte
Director, Corporate Sustainability & Responsibility,
Opportunity Sustainability
www.opportunitysustainability.com

Garry Schleifer, PCC, CMC
Publisher, *choice, the magazine of professional coaching*
www.choice-online.com

Beth Shapiro, MPA, PCC, CPCC, ORSC
Leadership & Team Coach
www.ssquaredassociates.com

Angela Spaxman
Career & Leadership Coach
www.spaxman.com.hk

Gopal "GD" Shrikanth, Columbia Certified Coach
CEO Coach, Mentor, Strategist
www.gd360.net

Rick Tamlyn, MFA, MCC, CPCC
Co-Founder, The Bigger Game®
www.biggergame.com

Zoran Todorovic, MCC
Founder, TNM Coaching
www.tnmcoaching.com

Frank Traditi
Executive Leadership & Business Coach
www.coachfrank.com

Dr. Stephen Treloar, MBA, M.ComLaw, DBA, MCC
Principal Coach, Coaching & Mentoring Australia
www.executive-coach.net.au

Jerri Udelson, MCC
Principal, Entrepreneurial Coaching & Consulting Svcs
www.jerriudelson.com

Rudy Vandamme
Coach Trainer, Researcher & Author
www.ecologize.net

Sir John Whitmore, PhD
Chairman, Performance Consultants International
www.performanceconsultants.com

Patrick Williams, Ed.D., MCC
Founder, Coaching the Global Village
www.coachingtheglobalvillage.org

Martha Willson, CPCC
Career Transition Coach
www.meaningfulwork.ca

ABOUT THE AUTHOR

••••••••••••••••••••••••••••

C.J. Hayden, MCC, CPCC, is a San
Francisco business coach who helps
her clients build enterprises
dedicated to social benefit and their
own right livelihood. C.J. is the
bestselling author of *Get Clients
Now!™*, *Get Hired Now!™*, *The One-
Person Marketing Plan Workbook,* and
over 400 articles on entrepreneurship, marketing, life
purpose, and social change.

As a pioneer in the coaching profession since 1992, C.J.
was a founding director of the worldwide Professional &
Personal Coaches Association (later merged with the
International Coach Federation). She was also the founding
editor of *Being in Action: The Journal of Professional & Personal
Coaching.* She has taught coaches and coaching for The
Coaches Training Institute and John F. Kennedy University.

As a citizen activist and social entrepreneur, C.J. is the
founder of the Send Girls to School Project and serves on the
board of A Good Deed Tea.

C.J. welcomes opportunities to speak with your group or
contribute an article to your publication about the ideas in
this book.

www.coacheschangetheworld.com

www.ingramcontent.com/pod-product-compliance
Lightning Source LLC
Chambersburg PA
CBHW060613210326
41520CB00010B/1319